PROBLEM SOLVING
IN A PROJECT
ENVIRONMENT

Problem Solving in a Project Environment

A CONSULTING PROCESS

L. THOMAS KING

A Wiley-Interscience Publication

JOHN WILEY & SONS

New York · Chichester · Brisbane · Toronto · Singapore

This publication is designed to provide accurate and
authoritative information in regard to the subject
matter covered. It is sold with the understanding that
the publisher is not engaged in rendering legal, accounting,
or other professional service. If legal advice or other
expert assistance is required, the services of a competent
professional person should be sought. *From a Declaration
of Principles jointly adopted by a Committee of the
American Bar Association and a Committee of Publishers.*

Library of Congress Cataloging in Publication Data

King, Landon Thomas, 1937–
  Problem solving in a project environment.

  "A Wiley-Interscience publication."
  Bibliography: p.
  Includes index.
  1. Problem solving. I. Title.
HD30.29.K56   658.4'04   80–20063
ISBN 0-471-08115-9

Printed in the United States of America

10 9 8 7 6 5 4 3 2

To my mother, who tried to get me to work hard

To my father, who tried to get me to work logically

To my wife, Ginger, who tries to get me to do either one

Preface

The process described in this book was developed from ideas collected on many projects on which I have worked with some excellent consultants. This consulting process is a synthesis from the many successful techniques tested on hundreds of projects.

I owe a special debt to Neil Tierney of Arthur Young & Company, who helped me get started on this subject several years ago. He encouraged me to continue developing this topic for our internal office use and contributed many key ideas to the process. In the formative stages of developing a training program for the Washington office of Arthur Young & Company, invaluable assistance was provided by Dick Connor of Synergy Corp. Dick conducted some workshops for us and provided some effective assistance in improving the methods that we used to conduct consulting projects.

The advice of my good friend Bob Hewitt has been most helpful. During our long discussions he helped me to clarify many elements of this process, especially those concepts discussed in the analysis chapter.

I would also like to acknowledge the unselfish contribution of ideas provided to me by Bev Lamont. Her conversations permitted me to improve my limited understanding of operations research.

The approaches described in this book are a consolidation of a host of techniques used on projects with numerous colleagues. I hope that my description of a way to conduct projects is an approximation of the techniques that I have used and that I have observed being used by some very talented colleagues. I accept full responsibility for the ideas presented and their integration into what I believe to be a systematic approach to solving clients' problems.

L. T. KING

Vienna, Virginia
November 1980

Contents

CHAPTER ONE

Introduction

S olving problems is an activity on which everyone spends a considerable amount of time and energy. Problem solving must be performed on an hourly or daily basis for most of our lives. Problems range from household difficulties to personal investment decisions to complex business problems. The emphasis of this book is on the formal problem solving projects in a business or government environment. Some topics discussed may have relevance for personal or other problems, but the approach described in the following chapters is not addressed to such situations.

Many problem solving approaches are used in managing projects. You have undoubtedly observed some people who seem to solve problems easily and some who seem to have a difficult time addressing the correct issues or completing any projects they begin. You may have observed some of the following types of problem solving approaches.

The Circular Approach. John is project manager on a project to develop and conduct a seminar for a government agency. He has made several loose assignments for several portions of the seminar. As the time for the seminar draws near, John is increasingly busy with other "important" work unrelated to this project and makes less and less time available to answer the rising number of questions from the staff that he has selected. When he does provide direction, the result is to have everyone scurrying in circles. The outcome of the seminar is predictable.

The Ostrich Approach. Bill is a project manager for the development of a complex information system for a government agency. As the staff develops more questions regarding the technical specifications and the interface with the client organization, Bill begins to attend fewer of the client meetings. When the client calls, he is more frequently tied up and asks someone else to return the client's call. He is desperately hoping the issues will be resolved by someone before he has to deal with them. This project also ends in mild disaster.

The Bull Approach. The design of a large inventory control system is nearing the stage when reports are due. However, the scope and content of what is to be provided to the client have not been defined. When the subject is discussed with Sam, the project manager, he responds with a forceful dissertation of the complexities and interrelationships of the project. The volume of his presentation becomes louder each time the subject is discussed but the substance of his presentation has not changed since the beginning of the job. He is trying to overcome project uncertainties with the force of his personality.

2

These stories probably remind you of dozens of projects you have observed in your professional career which were performed at less than optimum speed or resulted in less than satisfying results. This book addresses the need for, and an approach that can result in, more accurate and more efficient development of solutions to client needs.

1. WHAT IS PROBLEM SOLVING?

A problem may be defined as a question that involves doubt or uncertainty. There must be a choice among alternative courses of action for a problem to exist. If no decision is possible, doubt or uncertainty does not exist because the outcome will be a projection of the existing situation.

Many problems faced by decision makers involve a substantial amount of uncertainty, and the choices frequently are among "good" programs or ideas or among "bad" programs or ideas. If the decision making were restricted to a choice between the "good" project and the "bad" project, management's job would be much easier.

Problems can be formulated in a positive or negative manner. Ackoff (1978) described these as "the acquisition or attainment of something that is absent but desired" and "destruction, removal or containment of something that is present but not desired."

The project activity that results in solutions to client needs is composed of four basic types of inputs. These inputs are:

- A process for approaching the problem.
- Technical skills related to the type of problem being solved.
- Human relations skills that enable the project team member to effectively interface with the client, the data sources, and other members of the project team.
- The personal drive and motivation of the project team.

These inputs are depicted in Exhibit 1.1.

The generalized problem solving process described in this book is one way to approach the conduct of projects in a systematic manner. There is little, if anything, new in the various steps described. The process described is a way to conduct a project from beginning to end. The focus is overwhelmingly on

EXHIBIT 1.1   Inputs to Project Activity

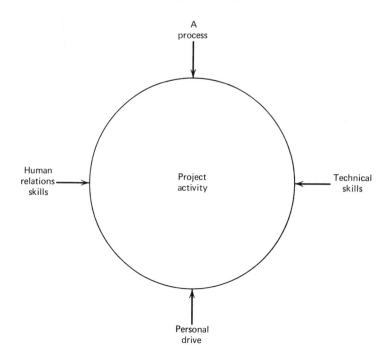

performing those actions, and only those actions, that directly relate to solving the problem the client retained you to solve.

This process is the result of a substantial amount of discussion and selection of ideas developed by the consulting staffs of the large public accounting, management consulting, and technical consulting firms, and from guidelines of the American Institute for Certified Public Accountants and the Association of Consulting Management Engineers. Much of the definition of this process was developed from experience in the Washington office of a large public accounting firm, and therefore an emphasis on government projects may be observed in the examples.

2. IMPORTANCE OF EFFECTIVE PROBLEM SOLVING

Most individuals and organizations need to resolve their problems in an effective manner to ensure that the correct problem is addressed and implementable solutions are identified. It is also important to proceed in an efficient manner to better ensure that the solution is obtained within available project resources.

The effectiveness of the project solution can be measured, ultimately, by whether the project recommendations are accepted and acted on. If the client does not accept and act on the project recommendations, the project team has failed. They have wasted the client's money and their time. There may be unusual circumstances where the recommendations are not acted on, but they should be rare occurrences.

Fortunately (or unfortunately, as the case may be) there are few places in this world where one can sit back and be unconcerned about improving the method by which he or she conducts business. It is hoped that by the use of this consulting process, productivity increases can be achieved by individuals and firms that address project-type problems.

In addition to worldwide pressure for increasing productivity, there is the companion problem of an increasingly complex world. In many cases, consultants are facing more complex systems in more complex environments and thus the process by which these projects are approached probably needs to be continually reassessed to determine if last year's approach is suitable for this year's problem.

3. GOALS OF THIS PROBLEM SOLVING PROCESS

When this description of a consulting process was developed, the following goals were established:

- Better quality results from consulting projects.
- Better control of the project activity by the individual staff member, the project manager, the firm management, and the client.
- Reduced time demands on the project staff and the project manager.

These three goals will be reviewed in the summary in Chapter 11, to describe how this process can achieve these goals.

4. INTENT OF THIS BOOK

The development and presentation of this description of a consulting process is directed toward:

- Management and technical consultants in private and government organizations.

- Engineers and other professionals working on projects.
- Managers buying, selling, or managing the conduct of projects.

The types of project used as a testing ground to develop the consulting process described in the following chapters, which I believe to be quite amenable to the use of this process, are:

- Consulting projects conducted for government clients by private consulting firms.
- Consulting projects conducted for industrial or commercial clients by private consulting firms.
- Internal projects conducted by government organizations.
- Internal projects conducted by commercial or industrial organizations.

5. AN UNDERSTANDING

This summary is an attempt to reach a clear understanding with the reader regarding what can be found in this book.

5.1. What Is Included?

This book includes:

- An overall description of a generalized process for solving problems.
- A step-by-step description of how this process can work.
- A case study describing a hypothetical project at each stage of the consulting process.

5.2. What Is Not Included?

The topics specifically *not* addressed in this text are:

- Project administration: organizing, invoicing, financing, providing support facilities, and so on.
- Project control, which includes those actions that need to be taken to ensure that the project is completed within the resource and time budgets.
- Contract administration, defined to include those formal documents,

letters, and conversations necessary to effectively control a consulting organization's liability.

- Detailed descriptions of any specific technical skills such as statistics and linear programming.

5.3. Resources Needed

The basic resources required to utilize the process described in this book are a reasonable amount of energy, motivation to perform good consulting work, and an open, inquiring mind.

The description of a consulting process in the next ten chapters is not the last word in problem solving and is not presented as the ultimate process. I believe that this description is a good synthesis of many of the most appropriate techniques now available to the international consulting community. I would certainly expect that improvements to this process are possible and will be forthcoming. In any case, this generalized problem solving process must be tailored specifically to an individual project. It cannot be applied in a "cook-book" manner to every client's situation.

It is my hope that this problem solving approach will allow each consultant, project manager, or buyer of consulting services to have an understanding of the general logic through which most projects should flow. This mental framework, I believe, will better enable the seller and the buyer of consulting projects to understand what should be done and to evaluate what has been done.

CHAPTER TWO

A Problem Solving Process

S olving problems in a project environment is a complex and demanding activity. Most of us can look back and think of times when we could have done a better job than we did. Our situation is somewhat like the farmer who sent back the latest publications he had received from the U.S. Government Printing Office with a handwritten note, "Please don't send me any more of these—I already know how to farm ten times better than I do."* Indeed, most people who are solving large or small problems really do not apply all of the relevant skills or knowledge that they possess to a particular problem in the most effective manner.

1. GOALS OF THIS PROCESS

The goals that were established to guide the development of the problem solving process are:

- Higher quality solutions and implementation plans that are achieved through earlier, more precise definition of the need that will be fulfilled. This permits a more effective allocation of available resources.
- Better control of projects by the client, top management, the project managers, and project staff. This better control results from a more accurate description of what needs to be done or has been done and the communication of those needs to the appropriate parties.
- Less time consuming on the part of project staff, project management, the firm's "top" management, and the client. This reduction in time results from more accurate channeling of resources to those actions needed to solve the basic problem—and only to those actions. Client and management efficiency results from more structured products being provided at defined milestones so that reviews may be more quickly accomplished.

These goals are reviewed in the summary in Chapter 11.

2. WHAT IS A PROBLEM SOLVING PROCESS?

An overview of the problem solving process described in this book can be pictured as a circle. The problem solving process (or consulting process) circle

*Donald Murr, "Management Information and Control Plan," *Arthur Young & Co. Journal,* 1968.

is presented in Exhibit 2.1 and consists of the following six phases:

- Identify the need.
- Plan the project.
- Collect the facts.
- Analyze the data.
- Develop alternatives.
- Present recommendations.

Let us briefly discuss each of these phases.

2.1. Identify the Need

It is critical for any project or other major activity to determine, at the beginning, exactly why the project is being conducted and what guidelines will be used to direct all subsequent activity. You have probably seen or been involved in projects where it became apparent at some point during or at the end of the project that there was a considerable difference of opinion among the staff members, and possibly between the consulting organization and the client, as to exactly what problem was to be solved. This first phase is simply a structured reminder to be sure that all parties involved in the project have a common understanding of what need will be satisfied by this project. The following basic activities should be performed to define that need:

- Diagnose the situation that led to the project.
- Define the need in clear, understandable terms; communicate this need; and obtain approval or concurrence from the project staff, management, and your client.

2.2. Plan the Project

A project effectively planned by precisely identifying the products to be delivered, the tasks to be performed, the milestones to be achieved, and the allocations of resources across the project has a significantly greater opportunity of (1) achieving meaningful results and (2) satisfying the client than a project that is planned casually. Everyone who has worked on projects has performed

EXHIBIT 2.1 The Consulting Process

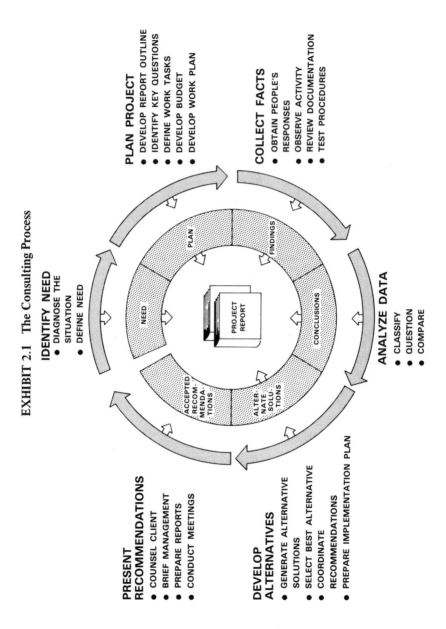

IDENTIFY NEED
- DIAGNOSE THE SITUATION
- DEFINE NEED

PLAN PROJECT
- DEVELOP REPORT OUTLINE
- IDENTIFY KEY QUESTIONS
- DEFINE WORK TASKS
- DEVELOP BUDGET
- DEVELOP WORK PLAN

COLLECT FACTS
- OBTAIN PEOPLE'S RESPONSES
- OBSERVE ACTIVITY
- REVIEW DOCUMENTATION
- TEST PROCEDURES

ANALYZE DATA
- CLASSIFY
- QUESTION
- COMPARE

DEVELOP ALTERNATIVES
- GENERATE ALTERNATIVE SOLUTIONS
- SELECT BEST ALTERNATIVE
- COORDINATE RECOMMENDATIONS
- PREPARE IMPLEMENTATION PLAN

PRESENT RECOMMENDATIONS
- COUNSEL CLIENT
- BRIEF MANAGEMENT
- PREPARE REPORTS
- CONDUCT MEETINGS

PLAN

FINDINGS

NEED

CONCLUSIONS

ACCEPTED RECOM- MENDA- TIONS

ALTER- NATE SOLU- TIONS

PROJECT REPORT

some *project planning.* Project planning is a method of providing a framework for orderly project activity. Project planning normally includes:

- Defining the specific end products to be delivered.
- Developing key questions to be answered.
- Defining the work tasks to be accomplished.
- Developing a work plan describing the planning results.
- Developing a budget of labor and other expenses for the project.

2.3. Collect the Facts

Efficient and effective fact collection is one of the most difficult actions in any problem solving process. A common difficulty is obtaining the data required to support the subsequent analysis and recommendations phases without expending an inordinate amount of project resources collecting data that will subsequently be found to be of little or no interest. The process that is described in later chapters will assist you to focus your fact collection and more easily limit your action to the facts required to respond to the statement of need you have now defined.

The principal activities used to gather facts are to:

- Obtain people's responses by the use of interviews, telephone surveys, or mail surveys.
- Observe the activity of personnel or systems that relate to the subject under study.
- Review documentation that relates to your situation.
- Test procedures of systems, or other processes, of your client or other relevant organizations.

The main purpose of the fact collection step is to allow you to collect sufficient data to be able to develop findings for the key questions that you identified during the planning process.

2.4. Analyze the Data

This phase consists of taking the data and the findings that result from the fact collection stage and reducing and analyzing this information to develop conclusions. The following activities are normally performed during analysis:

- *Classify* the data.
- *Question* the situation from many perspectives.
- *Compare* the data to your criteria or to accepted standards.

Numerous qualitative and quantitative analytical techniques are available to the modern problem solver.

The conclusions developed will direct the remaining study activity and provide guidance as to what kinds of alternative solutions should be considered.

2.5. Develop Alternatives

Begin developing recommendations by synthesizing the alternative solutions based on the need previously identified and the conclusions. It is important to generate and document many options that may be useful for providing a solution to the client's need. Several approaches may encourage the generation of innovative ideas. These alternative solutions developed should be defined, compared, and coordinated with your client to arrive at one or more recommended solutions to the basic need.

2.6. Present Recommendations

Rarely will anyone do anything just because you suggest he or she should. It must be demonstrated to each participant in the process that the implementation of an idea would be in his or her best interest. This requirement to communicate the importance and benefits of the recommended alternative is the driving force behind this phase. Careful consideration must be given to each of the clients involved in the project environment. Counseling, briefing management, preparing formal reports, and conducting general meetings for the broader client group are the methods normally used.

2.7. Provide Implementation Assistance

In addition to the six major phases that every project must go through, it is often advantageous for the client to retain the services of the project team to continue providing some support during the actual implementation of the recommendations. The extent of these services varies widely for different projects and for different client situations.

2.8. Evaluate Results

This phase, which is not employed as frequently as it should be, is that not-too-well-defined link between one phase of problem solving and the next. In most situations, a problem is identified and studied, and a solution is developed and implemented. Most changes that are introduced in any organization should be reviewed at periodic intervals to determine whether they are indeed satisfying the basic need for which they were implemented, and if so, to what extent. Therefore, it is good practice to identify, in the implementation plan for any project, the time period and the process to be used for conducting an evaluation of the effectiveness of that project. This evaluation should determine whether there are additional levels of detail that should be addressed once the first problem has been solved.

Thus the depiction of the consulting process as a circle has merit. Usually, with each trip around the circle the scope of the problems, and the degree of control of these problems, has been moved to a finer level of detail.

3. HOW DOES THE PROCESS WORK?

In this section the same process and the same phases of the consulting process just described are considered from a different point of view with concentration on deliverable products rather than actions and relationships. The process, as depicted in Exhibit 2.2, has defined output products for each phase.

3.1. Identify the Need

The identification of the need begins when a project is authorized, funded, and cleared to proceed. Usually this phase begins with the appointment of a project manager, and sometimes the key staff members. The first step in the identification of the need will be for the project manager to obtain copies of the principal documents to be used in initiating the project and place them in the hands of key staff persons and management. For a government contract, these documents would normally include the request for proposal, the proposal submitted, the contract, and other related reports, Congressional testimony, and other readily available material. After a quick review of these documents by the project manager, and possibly by other management officials or other people who may have been involved in selling the project but who will not be involved in the project activity, a meeting with the client's principal representative will be re-

EXHIBIT 2.2 Typical Project Documentation Flow
Page 1 of 3

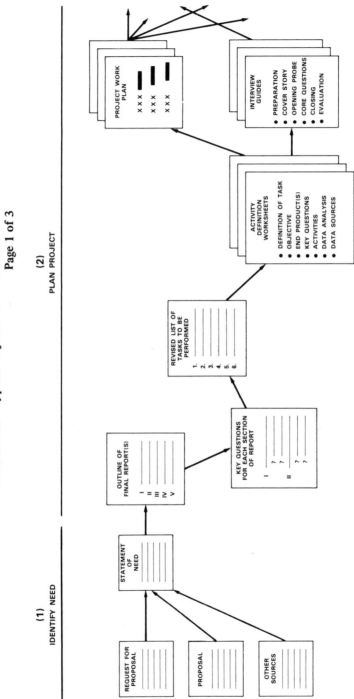

EXHIBIT 2.2 Typical Project Documentation Flow
Page 2 of 3

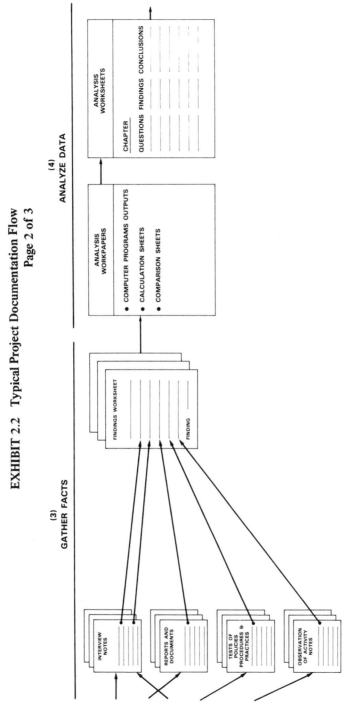

EXHIBIT 2.2 Typical Project Documentation Flow
Page 3 of 3

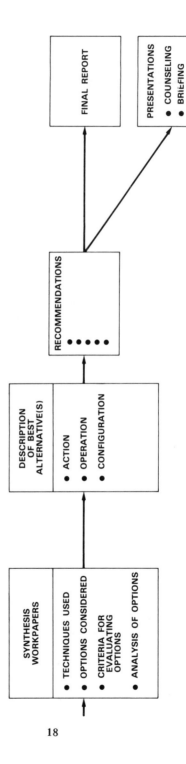

quested. At this meeting, certain open-ended questions will be asked to encourage the key client contact to provide insight into the reason for the project, assumptions that were made, constraints that the client is aware of, and other facts that it may not have been appropriate for the client to include in the formal request for proposal. Usually on the second or third day of the contract, after the client meeting (and after a review of the critical documents by several key project individuals), a meeting will be held with all the principal participants in the project. A consensus will be developed on exactly what the need of the client is. In other words, the problem to be solved will be carefully defined. This definition process will:

- List the issues to be resolved.
- Describe the assumptions included.
- Note the constraints the project must work within.
- Identify the principal clients for the project.

3.2. Plan the Project

Immediately after completion of the statement of need, the project team should outline the final report or reports. If at this time you know what problem it is that you want to solve, if you know what constraints and assumptions you must operate within, and if you know what clients are to be served, then you should be able to visualize the product needed at the end of the project to convince the clients that your recommendations should be followed. Immediately after developing a consensus on the outline of the final report, take the outline of each chapter of the final report and identify the key questions that must be asked and answered before that chapter of the final report can be written. These questions should be open-ended, nondirected questions that will lead the project team to a broad investigation of the topic.

The next planning step is to review the task list originally included in the request for proposal, the proposal itself, or both and determine if that list of tasks is still the most appropriate list and sequence of tasks required to be able to satisfy the need as defined.

The project team has by now performed a hard day's work and should pause until the direction they have established for this project is approved by management within the consulting organization and, subsequent to that, by the client. In most instances the review with the client at this time should be informal to allow a high level of interaction without getting involved in the formalities of the contract administration process. This informal review with the client could consist of (1) inviting the client by your office to look at your rough chalkboard or flip chart notes and discuss them with the project team, (2) taking the rough typed or rough flip chart copies of the material described above to the client and asking for his or her comments and concurrence, or (3) discussing the material with the client over the telephone. Usually a face-to-face discussion is preferable.

After management and the client have given their approval, the next step in the planning process is to define each task thoroughly. Each key staff person who has been assigned the responsibility for a task then could define that task more carefully. One way to do that is with an activity definition worksheet. These worksheets include a checklist for reviewing and defining items such as:

- The definition of the task.
- The objective of the task.
- The end products of the task.
- The major activities involved in the task.
- The data analysis techniques required.
- The data sources that will be used to obtain data for the task.

The next step in the planning process is to document the activity performed and the plans made during the planning process by developing a project work plan. The project work plan normally would include:

- The statement of need.
- The outline of the final report or reports.
- The key questions for each section of the report.
- The tasks to be performed.
- A description of all project deliverables.
- The data collection procedures to be used and the data sources identified.
- A project budget.
- A project schedule.
- A description of the responsibility assignments for each task.

This document should be a formal contract deliverable (a document defined in the contract as a formal product to be provided) and should be reviewed carefully by the firm's management. It should then be delivered to your client for review and approval.

Since most consulting projects are conducted on a fairly tight time schedule, often the development of interview guides will proceed in parallel with the development of a project work plan. The interview guides are necessary so that, for each of the interviews planned, the appropriate information will be obtained and the correct impression will be made on the interviewee. The appropriate impression is required because you are asking that person to take time and energy to respond to your request for information. Thus it is incumbent on the interviewer to be organized, to not waste the interviewee's time, and to minimize the need for having to go back a second or third time to get the information that the initial interview may have been able to provide. The stages in the interview process that must be considered, which are discussed in more detail in Chapter 5, are as follows:

- The preparation for the interview.
- The opening probe.
- The core questions.
- The closing.
- The evaluation of the results.

This completes the planning process and you and your project team are now ready to begin collecting facts.

3.3. Collect the Facts

The four principal methods of collecting facts are:

- Obtaining people's responses.
- Observing activity.
- Reviewing reports and documents.
- Testing policies, practices, and procedures.

For most projects the principal technique used to collect facts is interviewing. As earlier discussed, the interview is based on the interview guide developed during the planning process. The interview guide includes questions developed from the key questions identified during the planning process. The interview guide helps to ensure that the key questions will be covered and that the interview will be professionally conducted.

The observations of activity will be used for those questions requiring some measure of an operation or a group of employees. The range of detail that could be included in these observations is very wide. The details of the observation should be coordinated carefully with the client organization, and sound industrial engineering and personnel management techniques should be utilized. The results of the observation of activity would be the notes of the observer, structured in accordance with the key questions assigned and the organization of the unit being observed.

The review of reports and documents will also be conducted in accordance with the structure developed in the activity definition worksheets. These document reviews may be more efficient if specially developed worksheets for the project are used. Only that material in the documents which is related to the key questions that were assigned to the document reviewer will be highlighted or pulled out of the reference material.

The tests of policies, practices, and procedures will be conducted in accordance with the plan identified on the activity definition worksheet and normally will be conducted in conjunction with client personnel who may be responsible for the operation of the system being tested. In these tests, the documentation should include the key questions being addressed, a description of the system being tested, the input data, if appropriate, for the test, and the output documents from the system or procedure tested.

The next step during the fact collection stage is to assemble the facts from the many interviews and other data collection techniques to develop findings. This process can be enhanced by the use of a findings worksheet, as described in Chapter 5. The findings worksheet is simply a piece of paper that lists:

- The task being considered.
- The key question for which an answer is being sought.
- Relevant facts from interview notes, document review notes, the results of the tests of policies and procedures, and observation notes.

The facts will be selected and moved verbatim to the findings worksheet to support any question for which that fact is relevant. Each fact that is used has transferred with it the page number of the collection document from which it came. Thus each fact entered on the findings worksheet has an accurate audit trail back to its source.

Once the project manager decides sufficient facts have been transferred to the findings worksheet for a particular question, the task leader or the project manager will develop a finding for that question. A finding is defined as a simple, nonjudgmental sentence that answers the key question and provides direction to the subject under study. The finding is obtained by assembling a sentence from the exact words collected and transferred to the findings worksheet.

The completion of findings worksheets and the development of findings for each key question is a very important milestone for project management and organization management. It enables them to review the progress of the project team. In most projects the findings should be obtained at between 40 and 50 percent expenditure of project resources and time.

3.4. Analyze the Data

The data analysis phase is necessary to further subdivide and study the facts collected. The principal objective of the analysis step is to obtain conclusions regarding the meaning of the findings.

The analysis will vary substantially from project to project because of the technical nature of that particular project. The analytical techniques are generally categorized as qualitative or quantitative. Qualitative techniques would include such activities as:

- Asking basic questions.
- Searching for patterns.
- Developing forced relationships.
- Listing the attributes of the subject under study.
- Developing matrices.
- Developing reference projections.
- Visualizing how others might approach this problem.

The quantitative techniques would include such activities as:

- Cost analysis:
  - breakeven analysis.
  - incremental cost analysis.
  - opportunity cost analysis.
  - economic life.
  - return on investment.
  - present value.
  - cost benefit analysis.

- Modeling:
  - determinate.
  - stochastic (probabilistic).
  - time-based.
- Statistics:
  - descriptive techniques.
  - correspondence techniques.
- Presentation:
  - graphic.
  - tabular.

The categorization of techniques as qualitative or quantitative is not an exact demarcation. Many techniques could be either qualitative or quantitative. The categorization made is believed appropriate for consulting projects.

The output product from the analysis phase will be an analysis worksheet listing, by chapter outline, three columns. The left column contains the key questions structured as they are in the outline of the report, the second column contains the findings for the related key questions, and the third column contains the conclusions that relate to a single finding, or a group of findings, organized by chapter and subchapter headings.

3.5. Develop Alternatives

An important step in the development of recommendations is to synthesize alternative solutions for satisfying the defined need. This synthesis process will be structured along the lines that have been defined in the analysis stage just completed. The subjects receiving attention in the development of the alternative solutions are those topics suggested by the nature of the conclusions developed in the analysis phase.

After the initial identification of alternative solutions, these alternative solutions can be weighted and ranked. The most promising alternatives will be reviewed with the management of the consulting organization and subsequently with the key client personnel to obtain a high level of guidance and input on the structure and usefulness of each alternative.

The selected alternative to be recommended then will be defined. A recommendation should answer the following questions:

- What is prescribed?
- What are the benefits?
- Why is it important?

The recommendation may also provide answers to these questions:

- How can it be done?
- Who should do it?
- What resources are required?

3.6. Present Recommendations

The method of presentation of the recommendations to the client will have a large impact on whether the project is implemented. In most cases, if the consultant makes recommendations that are not implemented, he has failed. The net results are a waste of client money and a waste of the consultant's time.

Presenting the recommendations is a crucial action in obtaining the approval of and acceptance by the client management and the user officials of the recommended solution. A critical requirement at this step is to again analyze who in the client organization will be impacted by the recommended solution, how they will be impacted, and what is their probable response to this impact. Based on this analysis a communications plan may be developed for the presentation of the recommendation. These presentations usually include:

- Counseling key clients.
- Briefing management groups.
- Preparing a final report describing and supporting the recommendations.
- Conducting meetings with various user or other groups within the client organization.

Each of the steps summarized in this chapter is discussed in more detail in the next six chapters. In addition, implementing the project and evaluating the results are described in Chapters 9 and 10.

CHAPTER THREE

Identifying the Need

Identify Need

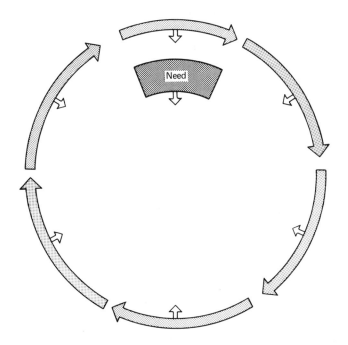

Need

W ould you believe that a person would drive from Washington, D.C., to San Diego before he realized that the real reason he came west was to do something in Seattle? It is obvious that if he had determined why he really wanted to go west before he left Washington he would have saved himself much lost time and resources. He would even have been able to correct his path with a limited amount of lost motion had he made the determination by the time he got to St. Louis (if he went that way).

Why do we conduct projects in such a fashion that we are figuratively to the California line before we ever figure out where we are going? This chapter focuses on some techniques for defining, at the beginning of your journey, where you are going.

One of the most important steps in any endeavor is to understand as early as possible what it is that you are setting out to do. In a structured project or contract situation, since there are usually time and resource constraints, it is even more important to define the need as precisely as you can as early as possible in the project.

1. THE PURPOSE OF NEED IDENTIFICATION

The purpose of pausing at the beginning of any project to identify and define the need is to develop a common understanding of the basic issues, constraints, and assumptions and to obtain client approval of this statement of need.

The development of a concise statement of need will enable the project manager to more effectively:

- Solve the correct problem.
- Focus project resources.
- Get management concurrence.
- Obtain client approval.

2. THE PROCESS (WHAT YOU DO)

What you may do to define this need will be discussed first and then how one can do it will be described. The actions that are recommended for a typical project are described below as a series of steps. These steps are depicted in Exhibit 3.1.

EXHIBIT 3.1 Identify the Need

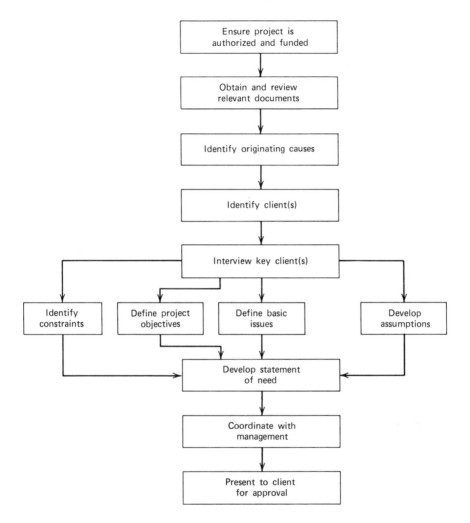

2.1. Begin the Project

One of the first steps that the designated leader of a new project must take is to ensure that the project is authorized and funded. For a private firm, this would include checking to see that the contract has been executed by both parties. In a government organization, this step would include obtaining clearance from the authorizing managers.

A very important early step in any project is the selection of the staff members for the project. In selecting the project manager and key project staff members, the total composition of skills should be considered. The larger the number of skills represented by the project team, the greater the number of considerations (or variables) that are likely to be identified.

If the different disciplines work in an interdisciplinary manner, with regular interaction of skills, the number and depth of the variables considered will likely be greater.

2.2. Obtain Key Documents

An early step in initiating a project is to collect the known, relevant, important documents for review by the project team. For a contractor to a government agency, the documents to be collected normally would include:

- The request for proposal.
- The proposal.
- The contract.
- Appropriate Congressional reports or other public reports.

If the project were an in-house government study project, the documents to collect might include:

- Formal directives.
- Confirming memos.
- Statutes or ordinances.
- Letters from other organizations.

Copies of these documents should be provided to each key member of the project team.

2.3. Identify Originating Causes

The basic motivating forces that caused the project to be conceived and funded should be identified early in the project. The causes may provide substantial additional insight into the issues to be addressed and the individuals or organizations that should be considered "clients."

Examples of what could be called originating causes follow.

- A large manufacturing company has retained a consultant to perform an organization study. After some discussions it was established that the overriding issue in the company was a struggle for power between the vice president for finance and the vice president for marketing. The split between them is causing the entire company to choose sides.

- A government agency has awarded a contract for a feasibility study for a management information system. Preliminary discussions determined that the agency director has been told by both Senate and House committee chairmen that the agency's legislative mandate and budget are going to be cut. Those impending actions will shape most activities of the agency.

- An established manufacturing firm has retained a consultant to review all scheduling of product runs in the factory. After due consultation, a major cause of the study was found to be extremely low morale among the production work force.

2.4. Identify Your Client(s)

It is important to review carefully who your client(s) is for the project. Sometimes it is clear who your client is because the client organization may be small and there may be one or two dominant individuals. However, most of the time there are multiple audiences to be understood. The multiple audience may include the client technical director who will monitor the project, client top management who must eventually approve the action recommended, operating personnel who will use the recommended system, people from other organizations who must interface with the system, and sometimes other political organizations and the public. You must initially determine which ones should be involved in developing or approving the statement of need and which ones should be involved in developing or approving the project recommendations.

The clients that should be involved in developing or approving the statement of need for the project usually include:

- The manager who initiated the request for the project.
- The manager who will have final authority to accept the project recommendations.
- The individual who will have day-to-day responsibility for guiding the consultants.

The second category, those clients who should be involved in developing or approving the project recommendations, usually includes several individuals in addition to the first category. The category could include:

- Individuals who will have to operate any system to be developed or reviewed as a result of this project.
- Individuals who will have to approve funds for implementation of the recommendations.
- Individuals who may be significantly impacted by changes that could result from the study.

The first category of clients should be identified accurately at this phase of the project. The second category should be identified as accurately as time and information will permit for project planning purposes, but changes to this second category will likely be made during the project.

2.5. Interview the Key Clients

It is necessary to conduct one or more preliminary interviews during the process of defining the need for the project to ensure that you more clearly understand the intent of the key officials. The three steps to be accomplished are:

- Develop a plan for each interview.
- Schedule the interviews.
- Conduct the interviews.

The planning for each interview should include: (1) checking on the protocol in that organization; (2) obtaining information regarding past, similar programs in the organization; and (3) preparing a list of questions to ask in each interview. The questions to be asked at this stage could include:

- What are the causes that generated the demand for this project?
- What issues need to be addressed?
- What assumptions have been made, or should be made, to conduct this project?
- What constraints exist that will shape the approach or the range of outputs from the project?
- What is the interviewee's definition of category one and category two officials that need to be interviewed and coordinated with?

- What are the interviewee's expectations regarding the output of the project?
- What are the interviewee's responses to your suggested study approaches?

The study approaches discussed might include the type and extent of data collection interviews, the types of analytical techniques under consideration, the kind and frequency of management briefings during the course of the project, and the methods of presenting the results.

After the planning has been completed, the interviews should be scheduled and conducted in accordance with the established protocol. (More discussion on interviewing can be found in Chapter 5.)

2.6. Identify Constraints, Assumptions, Major Issues, and Project Objectives

The need for establishing the constraints, assumptions, and major issues is obvious. If one begins to solve a problem without clearly identifying them, the project has a high potential for developing major difficulties.

The steps that can be used to develop the constraints, assumptions, and major issues include:

- Assemble the collective thoughts of the project team to determine:
  - what the client said the factors were.
  - what others said the factors were.
  - what the formal documentation indicated the factors were.
  - what the project team thought the factors were.
- Select the supportable facts from the data above.
- Apply the judgment of the project team.
- Formulate the constraints, assumptions, and major issues.

The constraints might include the following situations:

- The computer center hardware must remain because of the large dollar and status investment already made.
- Division X and Division Y cannot be merged because of the past experience with the personnel involved.
- The Tampa office cannot be closed because the chairman has his winter home there.

Conditions such as these can place real and rigid constraints on the conduct of your project. The constraints, which may be identified by the client or the consultant, represent a judgment about the boundaries of the project. Constraints identified at the beginning of a project are sometimes called arbitrary constraints. Constraints developed during the analysis phase to focus the problem are sometimes called derived constraints.

Assumptions might include such conditions as:

- The new organization plan will be based on the assumption that the merger between your client and Acme Machinery will be consummated.
- The implementation plan will be based on the assumption that Congress will extend the life of the agency for at least three years.

Major issues that could have an impact on your project should be identified; for example:

- Productivity improvements are needed to offset a declining amount of budgeted funds.
- Erosion of public and Congressional support places great pressure on the organization for achieving positive results quickly.

The project objectives normally should be defined in such a way that the definition is a clear statement of the expected direct output of the project. Examples of descriptions of project objectives are:

- The objective of the project is to prepare a report describing the feasibility of consolidating Division A and Division B.
- The objectives of this project are to design a management information system that serves the information needs of the three top levels of management of the agency and to develop a report describing the system.

2.7. Develop a Statement of Need

This step consists of consolidating the causes, client identification, constraints, assumptions, and major issues into a concise, coherent statement of the problem that is to be solved.

For some small projects this statement of need may consist of a simple list of topics to cover in a discussion with your client. For larger projects it could be a formal report, which could include project objectives, issues, assumptions, constraints, and key clients. In some cases it may be appropriate to include any originating causes in the report, but caution should be used in including some causes in a formal report.

Another concept that is sometimes useful is to identify the major parameters having an impact on the situation and to categorize the parameters into uncontrollable variables and controllable variables. The controllable variables may be divided into currently controlled variables and currently uncontrolled variables.

2.8. Coordinate with Management

After the draft statement of need has been fully discussed and concurred on within the project team, the statement should be provided to and discussed with the consulting organization management. This provides management with a good opportunity to review the quality of the results of the project team activity to date and to introduce the judgment of management into the definition of the problem to be solved. The coordination with management normally is more effective if the background and reasons for each of the major elements of the statement of need are actively discussed.

2.9. Present the Statement of Need to the Client for Approval

The statement of need should be discussed thoroughly with each major client to ensure that the project team has heard what the clients thought they were saying. The project manager, and often his management, should conduct these discussions with the client(s). It normally is helpful to provide a written statement of need to the client for his review, but it may not have to be a formal deliverable, just typed and dated. The client should review, approve, and concur that you are ready to begin the planning phase. (In many projects, the need definition may overlap the planning phase.)

3. CASE STUDY

To help clarify the consulting process described in this chapter and the succeeding chapters, a case study has been developed to provide a look at some practical examples of the application of this consulting process.

In this case study, a hypothetical project is described for each chapter, from Chapter 3 through Chapter 8.

The firm has a contract to conduct a feasibility study for the establishment of an independent security organization for a transit organization in a major metropolitan area. The contract for this study is valued at $75,000 and is to be completed in a six-month period. The vice president has assured himself that the contract is in order and has turned the project over to Bill, who will be the project manager. The first thing that Bill does is collect and carefully read the contract documents. In this case, the contract documents include the contract itself, the firm's proposal, and the request for proposal from the transit organization.

Based on the project organization structure proposed in the firm's proposal and discussions between Bill and the vice president, the key project staff members are selected. Bill then provides each of these key staff members with a copy of the contract documents and schedules a meeting in the conference room the following Monday morning.

During the period between now and the scheduled conference on Monday morning with the key project staff, Bill performs two very important tasks. He makes a preliminary search for additional relevant documents that may be useful in defining the problem at hand. The documents that he and the librarian were able to find are a study of another transit system security program in a distant city, legislative hearings regarding the security program for the proposed transit system, and two textbooks with relevant information for this study. As Bill's second task, he meets with the key client representative who will be monitoring the firm's work on the study and has a long discussion regarding the background, interests, pressures, and concerns of the organization about the security program.

On Monday morning at 9:00 A.M. Bill convenes the work session with Ed and Sally, his key staff members, in the conference room. The first hour is consumed by an open discussion, an exchange of ideas, and relaying the information that Bill picked up in his meeting with the client Project Officer. After each member of the team feels that he or she has a basic understanding of the project, the next step is to identify the objectives of the project. A consensus is finally reached on the objectives of the project by liberal use of the chalkboard and the flip charts to record and polish the many ideas discussed.

The next step that the project team takes is to identify the major issues involved in the project. This requires some sorting back and forth between the objectives previously stated and those topics that are now to be called issues. After the issues are generally agreed on, several constraints and assumptions for the project are identified and better defined.

The next step that the project team takes is to attempt to identify the major and minor clients involved in conducting a project such as this.

The project team now has the basis for a statement of need that will form the foundation for the entire study. They call the vice president and ask him to stop by the conference room for a quick briefing on their results to date in defining the problem. The vice president arrives in a few minutes, having previously been requested to set aside some time late on Monday morning for this purpose, and carefully discusses each of the foregoing topics with the project team. He asks several questions and adjustments are made in several items to reflect either a change in substance or a change in the tone of presentation. After completion of the review and after the project manager has positively asked of the vice president if he has further doubts about the definition of the project at that time, the group adjourns and Bill has a secretary transcribe the rough notes from the flip charts and the chalkboards and provide a typed draft to each team member.

Bill's next step is to take the rough notes from the working session and arrange for a review meeting with his principal client to discuss the objectives, issues, constraints, assumptions, and key clients to be addressed in the study. The working notes forming the statement of need for the project are presented in Exhibit 3.2. At first glance the items listed in Exhibit 3.2 may seem skimpy or

EXHIBIT 3.2   Case Study Notes—Statement of Need
Page 1 of 4

Objectives

- Determine feasibility of independent security organization.
- Develop implementation plan.

EXHIBIT 3.2   Case Study Notes—
Statement of Need
Page 2 of 4

Issues

- Public confidence.
- Cost.
- Legislative achievability.
- Interagency coordination.
- Ability to exert management control.

EXHIBIT 3.2   Case Study Notes–
Statement of Need

Constraints

- Multiple clients.
- Highly emotional issue.
- Limited prior interagency cooperation.
- Tentative political support for transit system.

EXHIBIT 3.2   Case Study Notes–Statement of Need

Clients

- The project officer.
- Transit organization management.
- Officials in the local police, fire, and rescue organizations.
- Officials in the legal community.
- Key officials in citizen organizations.

even simplistic, and that would be true if such a document had been prepared halfway through a project. However, the simple items listed, presented as they might appear on a chalkboard, developed at the beginning of the project can provide effective direction to the project.

4. SUMMARY

The development of a concise statement of need will enable the project manager to more effectively:

- Solve the correct problem.
- Focus the project resources.
- Get management concurrence.
- Obtain client approval.

The larger the number of skills represented by the project team, the greater the number of considerations (or variables) that are likely to be identified.

Most of the time there are multiple client audiences to be understood.

The statement of need would usually include the following:

- Project objectives.
- Issues.
- Assumptions.
- Constraints.
- Key clients.

CHAPTER FOUR

Planning the Project

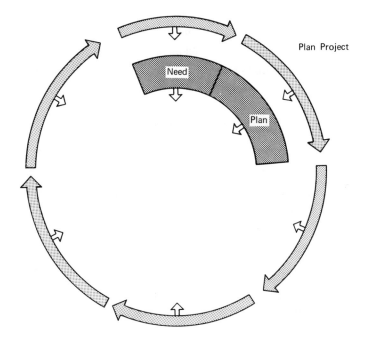

Have you ever seen a lonely, half-finished house along a back road that just seemed to shout out the pain and frustration of some well-meaning individual who began the project with great expectations, only to have it end in frustration because the cost or technical details had not been carefully planned?

How many of us have participated in projects that have not been structured well enough to keep people from running into each other, duplicating various activities, leaving serious gaps, and not really knowing when they were finished?

This chapter describes a method of laying a solid foundation for conducting a project.

1. PURPOSE OF PLANNING

The purpose of planning for the conduct of a project is:

- To direct study activity by focusing the project resources clearly on the need defined by the techniques discussed in Chapter 3.
- To achieve better communications of your planned activities and output products with your client, your management, and the project staff.
- To provide a mechanism for developing good control of the project.
- To develop a way to lower the contractual risks in most types of contracts.

2. RELATIONSHIP TO PROJECT CONTROL AND PROJECT ADMINISTRATION

The target of the planning activity described in this chapter is to focus project activity on developing a solution to the client's problem—to satisfy the need defined in Chapter 3. This planning will form a baseline for other necessary project activity such as project budgeting, project control, and project administration.

These three activities are not addressed specifically in this book. Perhaps it would be useful to bear in mind the definitions of these three activities in relation to the definition of problem solving, since all are directly related. My definitions are:

- *Problem solving:* The process of developing a solution to a situation that is of concern to your client.

- *Project budgeting:* The activities that are involved in allocating project resources across time, tasks, personnel, and expense categories.
- *Project control:* The activities that are involved in obtaining information on costs, activities, and output products, comparing the status of each to the approved plan, and taking corrective action if necessary.
- *Project administration:* The activities that are involved in preparing reports, preparing invoices, collecting bills, and completing internal reports, reviews, and forms.

3. THE PLANNING PROCESS

This section presents a step-by-step "cookbook" approach to planning a project. The process is generalized, and the reader will have to pick the steps and the emphasis appropriate for his or her project.

The planning phase may begin after the following steps:

- The statement of need has been defined.
- The client or clients have been determined.
- The key project team members have been identified.
- The statement of need has been approved by the client.

Five general steps that are often used in planning a project are:

- Outline each of the final products.
- Select the key questions.
- Review and sharpen the task descriptions.
- Develop a detailed work plan.
- Coordinate and obtain approval of the work plan.

The five steps are depicted in Exhibit 4.1 and are described in the following paragraphs.

3.1. Outline Final Products

This step describes a process for defining the form and structure of the final deliverable product(s) that will be required to convince the client(s) that the need has been fulfilled (or an action plan to fulfill the need has been developed).

EXHIBIT 4.1   A Planning Process

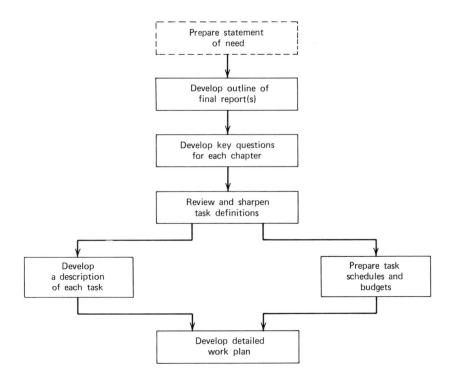

If you are not able to picture how you will need to tell your story to achieve acceptance of your recommendations at the end of the project, you probably do not understand the need or your client(s) well enough. This may require (1) that top management of the consulting organization get more involved at this point, (2) that the project team return to the need definition phase, or (3) both.

Some of the questions that will help organize the outline of the final report are as follows:

- Who will approve the final report?
- What will the approving official base the approval on?
- Who will use the systems or procedures that may be included in the recommendations?
- Will the using officials see the report?
- What will the using officials expect to see in the report?

- Who must concur with the recommendations?
- What should not appear in the report?
- Should there be an executive summary? (It may not be appropriate to address this question until the later stages of the project.)

A report will usually consist of:

- An introductory chapter that provides the purpose of the report and the current client situation.
- Three to five chapters describing the major subjects under study.
- A chapter presenting the recommendations and any necessary implementation plan.

The principal focus at this time, however, is to visualize the kind of information and the format that will be necessary to communicate to each of the clients that the project has been professionally conducted so that they will:

- Agree with the findings.
- Accept the conclusions.
- Act on the recommendations.

3.2. Select the Key Questions

Now that you have the basic outline of the final report, the next step is to begin the investigation with a very broad scope of inquiry by framing broad questions that will allow you to address the "*whole*" problem. This will help provide a hedge against jumping arbitrarily to a subset of the problem at hand.

For each chapter (and maybe subchapter) of the report, questions will be developed to help the project team understand the situation more fully. The questions developed will be those that must be asked and answered to permit the project team to write that chapter of the final report.

The most helpful questions are open-ended, nondirected ones which require the respondent to form a complete answer. These questions normally begin with:

- Who?
- What?
- Where?

- When?
- Why?
- How?

With a little practice, you can use these interrogatories as "idea generators" for the development of trial questions. After an initial effort at listing all the questions that come to mind for each chapter, it usually is necessary to go back over these questions, selecting those that are the "key questions" for each chapter. This selection process allows a quick focusing of the project on those lines of inquiry that are most relevant for your client's need, it is hoped, with little prejudicing of the results for those topics to be investigated. (I'm sure that each of you has seen a project in which unstated assumptions and limitations were placed on the possible outcomes by imprecise initial planning or by a drop to an inappropriate level of detail too early in the project. An example of this would be an information system study where the key project members got involved in input/output terminal selection before a thorough analysis had been made regarding whether or not the system should be automated.)

The final selection of key questions for each chapter will result in a list of questions that will focus all following project activity. The answers to these questions will assist the project team to:

- Establish the basic facts for the situation under study.
- Understand the significant relationships.
- Develop conclusions on major topics.
- Select topics on which to develop recommendations.

3.3. Review and Sharpen the Task Definitions

The end products of the project were noted in the previous section. This section describes a method for planning how to get from the plan to the end products, that is, the approach to conducting the project.

The method for planning the project tasks will vary substantially, based on the project that you are conducting. If it is a government contract, it is likely that there was a statement of work included in the request for proposal, a proposal that described the work tasks, and a contract that may also have included direction for the performance of specific tasks.

If the project is for a nongovernment client, the tasks may not be as well defined as for a government project. The nongovernment project may have been initiated by a series of discussions and a confirming letter. In such a case, the tasks may not have been described in a very detailed manner. This discussion is generally directed toward a government project.

A first step in planning for the tasks is to review the outline of the final report(s) and the key questions, considering the best way to ask the questions, analyze the data, and write the report. You can then begin from that base and build a set of tasks that are the most logical to you to achieve the project's objectives.

The definition of the tasks and their sequence will always be somewhat subjective based on the experience and interests of the person(s) doing the defining. There are, however, three ways that appear to be most common:

- Develop the tasks around the report outline.
- Develop the tasks around the skills and knowledge areas to be used on the project.
- Develop the tasks using an iterative combination of the preceding two approaches.

An example of a task structure that follows the outline of the report might look like this:

- Collect data on the current situation.
- Collect data on the information needed in the organization.
- Analyze the data and develop alternative solutions.
- Develop and present a recommended solution.

If the tasks were to be developed based on the skills to be used, the tasks might look like this:

- Study, review, and develop the overall information needs of the organization.
- Analyze the existing data processing capability and develop alternative methods of supporting the information system processing needs.
- Analyze the existing record system and develop the modifications necessary to achieve the desired end product.

Now that you have developed a series of tasks needed to accomplish the objectives of the project, you are ready to review the tasks initially described in the client's statement of work, the proposal, and other documents and compare these tasks to the task structure that you have just developed. If there are differences in the two sets of tasks, several questions could help sort out the differences:

- Is there a significant difference between the two sets of tasks?
- Is the difference significant enough to go through the process of obtaining management and client approval of the revised task list?
- Are the differences just "your way" rather than "someone else's way"?
- Will the revised tasks improve the project quality? How?
- Will the revised tasks result in a more efficient project?
- How will these efficiencies be obtained?
- How will the client benefit from these increased efficiencies?

After you are confident that you have acceptable answers to these and related questions, you are ready to develop the integrated task list that you will recommend to your client.

The next step is to coordinate these tasks with any management officials internal to the project team organization (partner, vice president, division manager, etc.). In most organizations, members of the management group have been selected because they have some experience and expertise in the subjects in which the firm does business. The project team should encourage the comments and direction that can come from higher level management. The management official who reviews the work of the project team must be receptive to newer techniques and different approaches and thus provide the project team some margin for creativity.

After adjustments have been made from the internal review, you are ready to seek concurrence of any task plan changes from your client. To expect your client to accept these changes, you should be prepared to tell (or imply to) him or her:

- Why the project results will be improved.
- Why the client personally will have increased stature, lower risk, and other benefits.

Client concurrence should be obtained before the project team expends the resources to develop detailed task descriptions.

3.4. Develop a Description of Each Task

After the task list has been completed and coordinated, the next step is to develop a description of each of the tasks to provide a detailed guide for the conduct of that task. This detailed planning should be done by the designated task leader if possible.

The detailed task planning should be directed to answering the following questions:

- What is the objective of the task?
- What is the end product of the task?
- What questions must be answered to accomplish the task?
- What activities are required to complete the work?
- What are the data sources?
- What are the data collection techniques?
- What data analysis techniques are required?

One way to conduct this task planning is to use a worksheet such as the Activity Definition Worksheet presented in Exhibit 4.2. The worksheet is designed to allow the task leader to think through the task in an orderly, efficient manner.

3.5. Develop a Detailed Work Plan

The purpose of developing a detailed work plan is to:

- Review the plan elements to be sure they are thorough and consistent.
- Provide a formal document for management and client approval.
- Provide a clear guide to the project team for the remainder of the project.

The work plan must be designed specifically for the project conditions, but generally it will include such items as:

- The statement of need previously developed.
- The outline(s) of the final report(s).
- A description of other items to be developed and delivered.
- The key questions to be answered.

EXHIBIT 4.2   Activity Definition Worksheet
Page 1 of 3

DEFINITION OF THE TASK

_____

_____

_____

1.   WHAT IS THE OBJECTIVE OF THE TASK?

_____

_____

_____

2.   WHAT IS THE END PRODUCT(S) OF THE TASK?

_____

_____

_____

_____

3.   WHAT QUESTIONS MUST BE ANSWERED TO ACCOMPLISH THE TASK?

_____

_____

_____

_____

_____

_____

_____

_____

_____

_____

_____

PREPARED BY	PAGE No. _____
DATE	
REVIEWED BY	OF _____
DATE	

EXHIBIT 4.2   Activity Definition Worksheet
Page 2 of 3

4.   WHAT ACTIVITIES ARE REQUIRED TO COMPLETE THE WORK?

_____

_____

_____

_____

_____

_____

_____

_____

_____

_____

_____

_____

_____

5.   WHAT DATA ANALYSIS TECHNIQUES ARE REQUIRED TO ANSWER THE KEY QUESTIONS?

KEY QUESTION No.	ANALYTICAL TECHNIQUE	SOURCE OF DATA

EXHIBIT 4.2 Activity Definition Worksheet
Page 3 of 3

6. INDICATE THE METHOD OF FACT COLLECTION THAT WILL BE REQUIRED TO OBTAIN
   INFORMATION. IDENTIFY BY KEY QUESTION IF POSSIBLE.

SOURCE OF DATA	DATA COLLECTION PROCESS			
	INTERVIEW	REVIEW OF DOCUMENTATION	TESTS OF PROCEDURES	OBSERVATION OF ACTIVITY
CLIENT ORGANIZATION	• Agency Management • Program Manager • Staff Personnel • Other Home Office Personnel • Other Field Office Personnel	• Statutes • Annual Reports • Congressional Testimony • Project Reports • Organization Charts • Regulations • Policy & Procedures	• Environment • Personnel Image • Work Plan • Product Quality • Management Controls	• Work Flow • Computer Programs • Control Systems
OTHER GOVERNMENT ORGANIZATIONS	• Officials with Related Functions • Officials Supplying Data to or Using Client Outputs	• Publications Used by Client • Description of Related Processes	• Comparability Observations	
CONSULTING FIRM	• Internal Functional or Program Area Specialists • Support Staff	• Reports • Proposals • Functional Skill Manuals • Home Office Library Support		• Reports of Other Tests
OTHER ORGANIZATIONS	• Academic Experts • Industry Specialists	• Trade Journals • Industry Standards		• Standard Processes

- A description of the approach to be used for each task.
- A schedule for accomplishment of each task and a milestone for completion of each major output product.
- An assignment of the individual responsible for each major output and task.
- A budget for labor, travel, and other expenses for the project.

Forms for a typical project work plan are presented in Exhibits 4.3 and 4.4. A project manpower schedule is depicted in Exhibit 4.3. It describes a typical project task by:

- Activity in the task.
- Person assigned to perform the task.
- Chargeable hours by time period allocated to the task.

The resources should be carefully scheduled across the life of the project to obtain an appropriate level of attention to each step. One method of obtaining a proper distribution of resources is to check your plan against the "law of fourths." This guide is to allocate roughly even amounts of project resources to:

- Planning.
- Data collection.
- Analysis.
- Report preparation and presentation.

A method of developing a project budget for a labor intensive project such as a consulting project is presented in Exhibit 4.4.

4. CASE STUDY

A few days after the initial meeting in which the project team defined the statement of need for the project, Bill, the project manager, arranges for another meeting of the project team. In the period since the last meeting, Bill discussed the preliminary statement of need with the client and had further discussions on project planning with the vice president. Each staff member has done some individual thinking about the project and has made steps to clear his or her calendar to be able to provide the necessary time to this project.

After a review of any comments that Bill received from the client or the vice

EXHIBIT 4.3 Project Manpower Schedule

CLIENT ORG._____   CLIENT OFFICIAL_____
PROJECT CODE_____   PROJECT MANAGER_____
PROJECT NAME_____   STAFF_____
NATURE OF WORK_____   LOCATION_____

ACTION	ASSIGNED TO														

EXHIBIT 4.4 Project Budget

PROJECT NAME _____

PROJECT CODE _____

CLIENT ORG. _____

DATE _____

STAFF	ROLE	OCT 15	OCT 31	NOV 15	NOV 30	DEC 15	DEC 31	JAN 15	JAN 31	FEB 15	FEB 28	MAR 15	MAR 31	APR 15	APR 30	MAY 15	MAY 31	JUN 15	JUN 30	JUL 15	JUL 31	AUG 15	AUG 31	SEP 15	SEP 30	TOTAL HOURS	DL RATE	DL COST
TOTALS																												

CONTINGENCY _____

TRAVEL _____

PRINTING/REPRO _____

MISC. _____

'' _____

TOTAL OTHER COSTS _____

OVERHEAD (%) _____

OTHER COSTS _____

SUBTOTAL _____

G & A (%) _____

TOTAL COSTS _____

PROFIT/FEE _____

TOTAL CONTRACT VALUE _____

**EXHIBIT 4.5   Case Study Notes
for Work Plan**

Draft Report Outline

1. Introduction.
2. Current situation.
3. Legislative considerations.
4. Security system alternatives.
5. Feasibility recommendations.

Appendices

A. Operational procedures.
B. Support systems and procedures.
C. Budget estimates.
D. Implementation plans.

---

president, and any new ideas or suggestions that the project team members have developed since the last meeting, the team focuses the discussion on those major topics that will have to be included in a final report for this project team to convey the recommendations and supporting material to the client. The goal used during the discussion is to structure this information to better enable the client to understand the recommendations and implement them. After much discussion and changing, shifting, and correcting ideas on the chalkboard and the flip chart, the project team agrees on the report outline indicated in Exhibit 4.5.

After they agree on the report outline, the next step is to immediately return to each chapter identified for the report and develop the key questions that must be asked and answered to be able to write that section of the report. Several questions for each section are identified and a sorting process is used to reduce the number of formal questions to be investigated to the key ones for that topic. A portion of the key question list is presented in Exhibit 4.6.

As soon as the project team reaches agreement on the key questions for each section of the report, they immediately begin to rethink the tasks, or action steps, necessary to carry out this feasibility study. They first develop a list of roughly defined tasks that will be necessary to answer the key questions. They compare this to the task list that had been presented to the client during the marketing period and in the firm's proposal. After resolving any differences between the two sets of tasks, the task list presented in Exhibit 4.7 is developed.

At this point during the meeting Bill again calls the vice president and asks him

EXHIBIT 4.6   Case Study Notes for Work Plan

Partial List of Key Questions

1. Introduction:
   - What is the purpose of this report?
   - Who is this report prepared for?
   - Why is this project being performed?
   - What elements will determine project feasibility?

2. Current situation:
   - What is the status of the current transit development plan?
   - What are the key issues involved in developing a security system for a transit operation?
   - What are the current political strengths of the transit organization?
   - What are the current political weaknesses of the transit organization?
   - What has been the history of cooperation among the many agencies involved in regional security?

EXHIBIT 4.7   Case Study Notes for Work Plan

Task List for Security Feasibility Study

1. Prepare work plan.
2. Organize regional committees for each service.
3. Develop operational resources requirements.
4. Develop administrative requirements.
5. Perform legislative requirements analysis.
6. Develop security system alternatives.
7. Perform feasibility analysis of security alternatives.
8. Present feasibility recommendations.
9. Develop recommendations for operational procedures.
10. Develop recommendations for administrative procedures.
11. Develop budget estimates for the recommended alternative.
12. Develop an implementation plan.
13. Prepare and present the final report.

to come by the conference room to discuss the report outline, the key questions, and the task list with the project team. The vice president is quickly able to determine whether this project team has a good understanding of what is to be provided to the client and a good grasp of how they are going to get there. After certain modifications and adjustments suggested by the vice president, the project team develops some assignments to be completed within a few days. One or more tasks are assigned to each of the project team members to develop a fuller description of exactly what each task would consist of and what resources will be required for that task. Bill will take the responsibility for coordinating the work of the various project team members and consolidating their outputs into a project schedule and a project budget. Examples of these are presented in Exhibits 4.8 and 4.9.

Bill's next step is to coordinate the rough outline and list of key questions with his client to be sure that the developing work plan is reflecting, as best it can, the work that the client wants performed. After incorporation of any relevant suggestions from the client, Bill then consolidates the planning documents into a project work plan. This project work plan includes:

- Statement of need.
- Report outline.
- Key questions.
- Task list.
- Project schedule.
- Project budget.
- Detailed task descriptions.

The work plan is finalized and presented to the vice president for review prior to submission to the client. The work plan is formally transmitted by letter to the client for his review, concurrence, and approval.

5. SUMMARY

The purpose of the project planning is to:

- Achieve directed study.
- Achieve better communications.
- Provide a mechanism for developing good control.

EXHIBIT 4.8 Case Study, Project Manpower Schedule

CLIENT ORG. __Transit Co.__
PROJECT CODE __4321__
PROJECT NAME __Security Feas.__
NATURE OF WORK __Feasibility Study__

CLIENT OFFICIAL __U. Catchem__
PROJECT MANAGER __Bill__
STAFF __Ed, Sally, Other__
LOCATION __City__

ACTION	ASSIGNED TO	OCT 15	31	NOV 15	30	DEC 15	31	JAN 15	31	FEB 15	28	MAR 15	31	APR 15	30
1 - Prepare Work Plan	Bill														
2 - Organize Regional Comm.	Sally														
3 - Develop Opnl. Rq'mts	Sally														
4 - Develop Admin. Rq'mts	Ed														
5 - Perform Legislative Analysis	Other														
6 - Develop Sec.Sys.Alternatives	All														
7 - Perform Feas. Analysis	Bill														
8 - Present Recommendations	Bill														
9 - Develop Opnl. Recomm.	Sally														
10- Develop Admin. Recomm.	Ed														
11- Develop Budget Estimates	Ed														
12- Develop Implemen. Plan	Bill														
13- Prepare Final Report	All														

59

EXHIBIT 4.9 Case Study, Project Budget

PROJECT NAME __Security Feasibility__ CLIENT ORG. __Transit Co.__

PROJECT CODE __4321__ DATE __5 Oct 19XX__

STAFF	ROLE	OCT 15	OCT 31	NOV 15	NOV 30	DEC 15	DEC 31	JAN 15	JAN 31	FEB 15	FEB 28	MAR 15	MAR 31	APR 15	APR 30	MAY 15	MAY 31	JUN 15	JUN 30	JUL 15	JUL 31	AUG 15	AUG 31	SEP 15	SEP 30	TOTAL HOURS	DL RATE	DL COST
Bigman	VP	4	4	4	4	4	4	4		4		12	12													40	$31.45	$1,258
Bill	PM	50	40	40	40	40	20	30	–	40	50	50	40													420	20.96	8,803
Ed	Data	30	20	20	–	30	–	40	50	50	30	20	10													300	18.34	5,502
Sally	Secur	24	16	40	40	50	50	–	40	60	40	40	40													420	15.72	6,602
Other				20	40	20	–	20	20	20																120	14.00	1,680
																									TOTALS	**1,300**		**23,845**

OVERHEAD (120%)	28,614
OTHER COSTS	8,400
SUBTOTAL	60,859
G & A (12%)	7,303
TOTAL COSTS	68,162
PROFIT/FEE	6,838
TOTAL CONTRACT VALUE	75,000

CONTINGENCY	$ 4,000
TRAVEL	2,000
PRINTING/REPRO	1,000
MISC.	1,400
"	
TOTAL OTHER COSTS	8,400

- Develop a way to lower the risks to all parties.

The five general steps that are recommended for project planning are:

- Outline the final products.
- Select the key questions.
- Describe the tasks.
- Develop a work plan.
- Obtain approval of the work plan.

The project work plan typically will include:

- The statement of need.
- The outline of the final report.
- The key questions.
- Task descriptions.
- A schedule.
- Assignments of task responsibility.
- A budget.

CHAPTER FIVE

Collecting the Facts

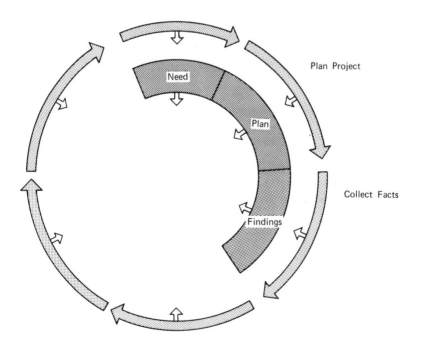

Identify Need

Plan Project

Collect Facts

Need

Plan

Findings

H ave you ever participated in or observed a group of people collecting data that reminded you of a platoon of Charlie Chaplins bouncing off each other in a confused manner? Projects frequently are conducted in this fashion with the personnel involved collecting large amounts of data and then, at the end of the project, trying desperately to assess which of the data that they have collected are relevant, and where the relevant data are located in the ton of materials that has been collected.

Almost any project (a problem solving process) deals with the unknown and thus there will always be a degree of uncertainty and inefficiency in the collection of the data. This chapter is directed toward describing a process that can improve the effectiveness and efficiency of the data collection process.

1. PURPOSE OF FACT COLLECTION

A principal focus of the fact collection phase is to obtain enough facts to be able to answer the key questions. This answer will be in the form of findings. A finding is defined as a simple, nonjudgmental sentence which answers a key question and provides further direction to the subject under study.

A supporting purpose of the fact collecting process is to establish a data base that is relevant to the project under study. In almost any topic that one gets involved in, there are mountains of data available on the general topic of the subject under study. It is most important to be able to select among these data for the data elements that impact, or impinge on, the major issues. This could be compared to separation of precious gem-bearing stones from tons of rocks. It is obviously very important to perform this as efficiently as possible. In some highly quantitative projects, the development of an organized data base for use in later analytical stages is also a purpose of a fact collection process.

2. SCOPE OF FACT COLLECTION

The collection of facts is that phase in the process between the completion and approval of the work plan and the beginning of analysis. With the understanding that project problem solving is a series of miniprojects at various stages in the project that require an almost complete consulting cycle, the following description is presented as a simple description of the fact collection phase.

2.1. What Is Included?

The fact collection process includes several steps. The most prominent of these are the following.

Finalize the Data Collection Plan

During the Development of the work plan described in Chapter 4, considerable thought was given to the methods that would be used for collecting facts. Four basic techniques generally used to collect facts are as follows:

• Obtain people's responses.
• Observe the activity of people and systems.
• Review written documentation.
• Test working procedures and systems.

For a particular project, the balance necessary among the four data collection techniques was discussed, reviewed, and approved during the planning process. At this time, the beginning of fact collection, these processes need to be considered again carefully while the detailed data collection plan is being developed. The detailed data collection plan will be a fairly specific plan for how to accomplish the following steps.

Complete the Guides

Each of the four techniques just listed will require a specific guide for the conduct of an interview, a telephone survey, a mail survey, a review of documentation, an observation of activity, or a test of a procedure. In some instances an interview guide may be put together quickly and informally for a face-to-face interview. It may be a structured, typed document or it may be a concurrence among the project team as to which questions will be picked up and asked by each interviewer of each interviewee.

For mail surveys the development of the mail questionnaire is normally a complicated process requiring careful drafting, interim reviews, and tests of the draft questionnaires.

Scheduling of Data Collection

In many cases, careful coordination with client and other organizations is required to select the time, place, and the specific interviewee, or process to be reviewed.

Collecting the Data

Obviously the bulk of the time during the fact collection step is the actual collecting of the data from several sources. This collection is discussed in more detail later in this chapter.

2.2. What Are the Limits?

The beginning of data collection (or those things that should be accomplished prior to the start of data collection) should be based on the following items:

- An approved project report outline.
- An approved list of the key questions by section of the report outline.
- An approved project task structure.
- An approved data collection concept.
- An approved data collection and analysis budget.

Until these items are completed and in the hands of the project data collection team, formal data collection probably should not begin.

A second limit (at the end of data collection) involves the decision that enough data have been collected and that these facts can now support the remainder of the project. The best way to determine when data collection has been completed is a review of the findings worksheets that have been developed for each key question. If the judgment of the project staff member, the project manager, and/or the manager/partner is that enough facts have been assembled and transferred to findings worksheets to enable a supportable and reasonable finding to be drawn from those facts, then data collection is completed.

In this book the word "fact" and the word "data" are used in many discussions. Although they are essentially identical, one difference used here is that the term data generally is used to describe a broader universe of information elements than facts. Facts are generally considered to be those data elements that are relevant to the specific problem under study.

3. METHODS OF FACT COLLECTION

This section is an overview of the principal fact collection techniques used in management consulting projects. The overview is provided so that anyone involved in projects will have enough familiarity with the various techniques to understand how they relate to the overall problem solving process. Sources of additional information on any of the techniques may be obtained by referring to the bibliography.

As indicated in the preceding sections, the four principal techniques for fact collection are to obtain people's responses, observe activity, review documents, and test procedures. The steps in each technique are presented in Exhibit 5.1. Each of these techniques is described below and an indication is made of their uses, advantages, and disadvantages.

3.1. Obtain People's Responses

Collecting facts by asking people questions is divided into three categories:

- Direct face-to-face interviews.
- Telephone surveys.
- Mail surveys.

After the three techniques are discussed, the use, advantages, and disadvantages of each technique are summarized.

Interviews

The collection of facts by interviewing is probably the most widely used and important fact collection technique. There will be projects where other techniques are used more extensively on that project, but in the course of many projects conducted by an organization, the interviewing process is likely to be the key technique used. Interviews are used to collect judgments, specific information, and general information from selected interviewees.

The activities involved in a typical interview include the following:

Prepare an Interview Guide. The interview guide will be based directly on the key questions developed during the project planning phase. (The guide is sometimes called an interview schedule but interview guide is used in this book to avoid confusion with scheduling interviews.) Those key questions and appropriate supporting questions will be developed and the questions will be allocated to the various interviews to be conducted. These questions may be distributed on typed, formatted interview guides or, once the questions to be asked are agreed on, they may be included in the margins of interview forms so that the questions and answers may be easily collected on the same sheets of paper. Exhibit 5.2 is an example of an interview guide.

EXHIBIT 5.1 Collecting the Facts
Page 1 of 2

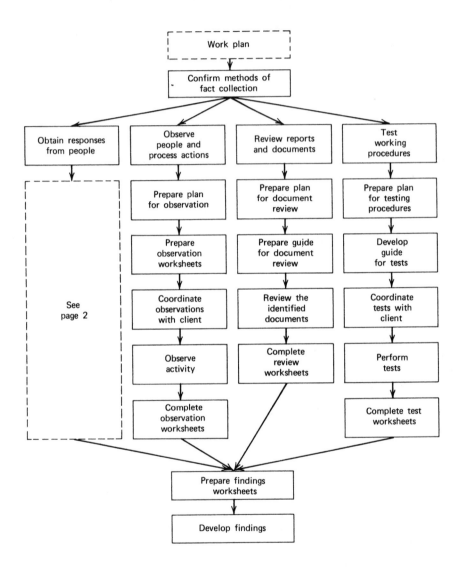

EXHIBIT 5.1 Collecting the Facts
Page 2 of 2

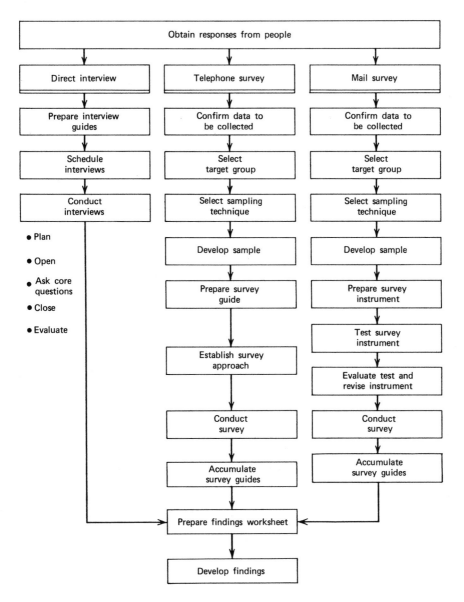

Note: For projects that require the collection of extensive data, it may be necessary to use quantitative analytical techniques at this step.

EXHIBIT 5.2   Interview Notes

	TASK No. _____	INTERVIEWEE _____
INTERVIEW NOTES	No. _____ _____ _____	ORGANIZATION _____

KEY QUESTIONS OR TOPICS	INTERVIEWEE RESPONSE	INTERVIEWER COMMENTS

PREPARED BY ___ DATE ___
REVIEWED BY ___ DATE ___
PAGE No. ___ OF ___

Schedule the Interviews.   During the planning process an analysis was made of the number, types, and possibly the individuals to be interviewed. This subtask involves scheduling those interviews for which the interviewee has been identified by name, or identifying appropriate individuals within the organization to be interviewed and firmly scheduling those interviews.

Careful consideration should be given to the time, place, and conditions of the planned interview. In many cases it is difficult to get an interviewee to be informative on a complex subject if the interview is 8:00 A.M. on Monday, at 11:00 A.M. when the person has an important luncheon to attend, or at 4:30 P.M. if the person rides in a car pool. Some people might prefer an interview in the later afternoon and might actually be more informative after most of their office staff have gone home.

If you have difficult questions to ask and you know that the person to be interviewed has a phone ringing constantly or has other disruptive activities in his office, try to arrange for the interview in a nearby conference room.

It is normally a good idea to have a one-on-one interview situation. The interviewee is usually relaxed and informative in this situation, without the "interrogator-witness" image of a group of interviewers. The one-on-one interview is also less expensive for the consulting organization than having two or more interviewers.

Sometimes it may be appropriate or necessary to conduct an interview using two interviewers. If you are asking for a lot of quantitative data, two interviewers may be useful. If conditions develop where an interview is clearly going to be an adversary process, then it may be necessary to have a second person present to witness what was said. This type of interview situation places pressure on the interviewer to ask the correct question since the interviewee is not likely to be expansive.

If there are two interviewers, one should be designated, in advance, as the one to ask questions and the second to be the principal note taker. The note taker should get involved only to ask follow-up questions, generally late in the interview. This approach is recommended because if two or more interviewers are asking questions, (1) it is difficult to establish rapport with the interviewee, (2) the line of questions probably will not be continuous since the questioners may follow different thought trails, and (3) the interviewee may become defensive.

Two interviewers are often used in interviews such as criminal investigations where the interviewers are in almost total control of the interview. They are less useful when the interviewee can invite you to leave, and be rid of you, at any time.

Situations will arise when one interviewer will be faced with more than one interviewee. This is a difficult situation for the interviewer since it becomes very hard to take accurate notes and get the proper attribution. It is sometimes useful to have more than one interviewee when the primary objective is to contact large numbers of middle-level personnel, permit each to make a contribution, and allow the consultant to begin to provide information and insights that might permit the interviewees to better understand the project objectives. This better understanding may cause the interviewees to develop more confidence in the project approach and be more inclined to act on the recommendations.

The typical interview length should be kept down to 30 to 50 minutes if possible. This places some pressure on both the interviewer and interviewee to be precise and minimize irrelevant discussion. Thus interviews should usually be no more frequent than one an hour, but every 90 minutes is preferable.

Conduct the Interviews. The interviewing process may be described by breaking it into five stages:

- Planning.
- Opening.
- Asking core questions.
- Closing.
- Evaluating.

Each of these stages is briefly described below.

PLANNING. The planning for a specific interview will include several activities. The major activities in the planning process are:

- Establish the specific objectives for this interview. This means identifying either in writing or mentally the results that you would like to achieve from the questions you will ask and the discussion you will have with this interviewee.
- Determine the known information you have already collected that is relevant to this interviewee. If this the first interview, then this activity may be less important. If it is a later interview, you have already conducted a number of interviews or other data collection activities in this or related organizations, and thus have a substantial amount of information about the organization. If you proceed to ask everyone in the organization the same questions, you may be wasting their time, your time, and the client's money. You should make a specific determination on whether you have enough information on any subject. If you are satisfied with the information already collected on that particular subject, then that subject should be deleted from the interview guide for subsequent discussions.
- Determine and define the specific information needed from this inter-

viewee. This action is related to the preceding activity and provides a measure for increasing the efficiency of the interview process.

- Be sure that you have the interviewee's name, title, and organization clearly in your mind. It is not very impressive for an interviewer to come into an interview situation knowing little or nothing about the person with whom he or she will be talking.

- Review the interview guide to be sure that it specifically will respond to the activities just described. If any significant period of time elapsed between the initial scheduling of the interview and the time the interview is to be conducted, call and confirm the interview date, time, and location.

OPENING AN INTERVIEW. The opening phase of an interview is very important to determining its overall productivity. The first thing that the interviewer should do is to introduce himself or herself very clearly. Interviewees will not be impressed if they have to stumble through the rest of the interview period without being sure of the interviewer's name.

It is equally important in an interview to establish a high level of eye contact immediately and retain, during the course of the interview, as much direct eye contact as the interviewer can manage. The eye contact will be useful in getting the interviewee involved in the discussion and will enhance the establishment of rapport between the interviewer and the interviewee.

Encourage the physical positioning of the interviewee to minimize the mental barriers to communications. If the interviewee is looking across a cluttered desk filled with half-finished projects, every time he looks at you he notices another unfinished project. His mind may repeatedly jump to those projects. In addition, he may resent the time spent with you as extra time it will take that evening to complete his day's work before he goes home. If at all possible, encourage the interviewee to move away from his desk into a separate chair arrangement in the office, if possible, or to move to a conference table or a seating setup that minimizes outside interferences. If there is a conference table, try not to sit directly across the table from the interviewee. Sit on a table side 90 degrees from the interviewee, or even sit on the same side. Try not to sit in an adjacent chair if the chairs are very closely spaced, since this may penetrate the "personal space" and make the interviewee unconfortable.

After you are introduced and seated, the next thing that the interviewer should do is present a clear and consistent cover story. The cover story is a short, clear description of the purpose and scope of the project. The cover story should be prepared by the project manager and adhered to very closely by all the interviewers on the project. If Interviewer A talks to the division director of Division A and says that this is a requirements analysis for a management information system and Interviewer B talks to the director of Division B and states that this is an organization study to look at management's needs, when Division A director and Division B director compare notes they will be less than impressed with the quality of the personnel performing the study.

The next step is to verify the information that is to be requested during the course of this interview. This is important because it lets the interviewee focus on the scope of the questions that he will be asked during the course of the interview. It also allows the interviewee to relax and concentrate on the subjects he now knows will be discussed. If all you need from this person is information regarding his organization's requirements for data processing, and the interviewee sits there through the entire interview "sweating blood" over whether, and when, you are going to ask a question regarding this painful personnel problem in his organization, he may go through the entire interview giving defensive and less than helpful answers to your questions.

The last action in the opening stage is to provide a transition to the core questions of the interview with what is called a scoping probe, a nondirective general question that leads off with who, what, where, when, why, or how and relates to the organization or operations of the interviewee's group. This question should be easy for the person to answer and should establish the tone of the interview so that the interviewee will feel more disposed to freely answer subsequent questions.

CORE QUESTIONS. These questions focus on the central purpose of the interview and are the heart of your fact collection activity. The most usual technique is to use open-ended, nondirected questions. These questions usually begin with who, what, where, when, why, or how and place the responsibility for providing form and boundaries in the response on the interviewee. They are particularly well suited to exploratory questioning where you think there may be related topics of interest to you but you're really not quite sure what those topics are. It is the responsibility of the interviewer to frame the nondirected question so that the respondent must structure the answer while at the same time not asking the question in such a way that the respondent gives a 30-minute response to each question.

To follow up on the points requiring clarification and to close the interview by obtaining specific data that you think are available in this organization, the interviewer usually will ask directed questions. Directed questions—usually beginning with do, shall, did, can, may—put the responsibility on the interviewer to present an accurate, well-structured situation. Directed questions may permit the respondent to answer yes or no. The problem with asking and answering questions has been highlighted by the story regarding the two people who were lost in a balloon floating in the clouds. During a small break in the clouds, they saw a person down below on the ground—whereupon one of the balloonists leaned over and yelled, "Where are we?" to the individual on the ground. The response was, "You're in a balloon." One of the balloonists turned to the other one and said, "That person is a lawyer." When the other one asked why, the answer was, "He gave us a technically correct but totally useless response."

It is also important for an interviewer to conduct himself or herself and frame the questions in a way that will not prejudice the response. You may distort a response by your mannerisms or your conversation if the interviewee infers that the interviewer holds a given viewpoint. The interviewee may provide incorrect or incomplete information about the situation, especially if the interviewee believes a study of his organization is a threat to his job, believes you will report his comments to his supervisors, feels that the interviewer is overbearing, or is unduly concerned over the influence that you may have with his supervisors. For example, by asking "Do you believe the output products from the headquarters data processing center are obsolete?" you have just said that *someone* thinks the products are obsolete.

An alternative way to obtain the information might be: "What products do you receive from the headquarters data processing center?" "How do you use the products? How could they be changed to make them more useful to you?" A line of questioning such as this would permit you to get an uncontaminated response from the interviewee, which would be a much more valuable fact.

Be alert for "handles." Handles are those statements or bits of information coming out of a discussion that beg for a follow-up question to solicit further clarification. The interviewer must decide whether to respond to the handle immediately or whether it would be more productive to delay until later in the discussion and come back to that subject through the use of a different question. For example, you are discussing the organization study with the executive vice president and as a casual comment he happens to drop, "as long as Department 23 exists. . . ." If Department 23 figures at all in your organization study and there is doubt in the vice president's mind as to whether that department will continue to exist, then that is an important point that the interviewer should clarify, if possible, before the interview is over.

After a general response made by the interviewee, ask for a clarifying example. These clarifying examples will help to reduce the possibility of a missed communication during the interview.

Be alert for multiple messages. People frequently respond using words that are perfectly appropriate for the question. Sometimes, however, the tone of voice or the body language that is used might suggest that there is another meaning to this response. Usually it is more appropriate to probe gently to attempt to obtain additional understanding of the potential multiple messages involved. A soft probe uses a very general, nondirected question that does not address the issue of interest directly. Consider again the Department 23 situation just discussed. You might follow up with: "What organizational realignments have been discussed for the next three-year period? What types of realignments may be likely in the next three years? A hard probe would be: "What did you mean when you said, 'As long as Department 23 exists'?"

The product of your interview will be your interview notes. This is your permanent record of what transpired during the interview. It is most important that you take accurate notes quickly. This is always a problem for the interviewer since the quality of the interview usually is directly correlated with the amount of eye contact that the interviewer maintains with the interviewee. This places a requirement on the interviewer of taking notes while looking the interviewee in the eye for substantial periods of time. Suggestions for note taking include developing a strict personal guideline of only writing down the actual words that the interviewee said. It is most important that the interviewer document the words stated by the interviewee; if you use other words, there is a possibility that you already have made a translation of what the individual actually meant. Moreover, if you, however unfortunately, are called upon to testify about the veracity of the information you used as a basis for your study and you cannot clearly state that all or essentially all the words that appear in your interview notes are those actually used by the interviewee during the interview itself, then your reputation, and possibly your pocketbook, may be adversely affected.

Additional guides for note taking include making headlines of major subjects and indenting those subjects with bullets (dot points) so that, although you may only write a verb and a noun, at least you have the proper relationship of the actual thought process of the conversation. To enhance your ability to do this, don't crowd your interview notes. Leave a large amount of space as you move down the page.

Take your notes with a pen. It is most important that the interview notes be recorded in a permanent handwriting on good paper. Taking notes in pencil does not provide a high-quality audit trail. Notes written in ink are more difficult to alter after the fact. Some of you may concur, as I do, with those who say that the interviewer is better received, and held in higher esteem, by the typical interviewee if an expensive pen is used.

Many consultants believe that white 8½ x 11 inch lined note pads are preferable for recording interview notes for most situations. There are situations where other types of note pad are more appropriate.

It may be appropriate to use an 8½ x 14 inch yellow audit workpaper pad if you are talking to the assistant controller about financial data. If you plan investigative interviews, which may be required for a project to study a bank failure for the Controller of the Currency, then 8½ x 14 inch yellow legal pads may be appropriate. The legal pads remind many people of lawyers and the law—if that's the frame of reference that you want the interviewee in, then it's a good tool.

The use of tape recorders for interviews may be appropriate for some circumstances but there are few interviewees who will talk as freely when they are being recorded as they will without a recorder. Recorders are often used in investigative interviews to provide an accurate record of the conversation. The interviewees often have little choice in controlling the interview techniques.

Recorders are also used frequently in news interviews. The interviewer also has an edge over the interviewee since the interviewee often wants the publicity associated with a news broadcast or is concerned about how the interviewer might report on an "uncooperative" interviewee.

However, for the typical interview situation when the interviewer is requesting information from someone who doesn't have to cooperate, the use of audio, or video, recorders is not recommended. If you have exploratory questions to ask, the use of recorders will increase the probability of not obtaining some key information.

The major point is that the tools, dress, and bearing of the consultant have a strong influence on the interviewee and the answers that will be provided. The consultant should make a positive decision regarding the impression that will be made. A man may wear a dark blue pin-stripe vested suit with a white shirt and dark tie or he may wear casual clothes but he had better be aware of the impact. For a further discussion of dress, refer to Molloy's *Dress for Success.*

The interview guide is useful during the interview for providing the interviewer an easy method of recording which of the questions are being answered. The guide allows the interviewer to freely slide into the next question and move the questions around to reflect the flow of the interview. The guide is particularly useful to indicate to the interviewer that all the core questions have been asked, and answered, and that the core question part of the interview is completed.

CLOSING. Clearly indicate to the interviewee that the interview is over. In many cases, in tension-filled organizations or officials, you can literally see the interviewee relax when you convey that the tough questions, or potentially tough questions, are over. Some interviewers attempt to sometimes slide in a hooker of a question during the closing of an interview, after the person has relaxed, to obtain sensitive information that they do not feel they might otherwise have obtained. If a technique such as this is used, it must be considered very carefully in advance. There can be strong negative feelings generated by an interviewee who feels that he has just been outfoxed. If the interviewer has additional business in that organization, cooperation may evaporate quickly.

Thank the person for cooperating. He or she has just taken a period of time out of a busy schedule to respond to your request for information, doing you a favor by trying to provide you with the answers you seek.

Obtain permission to contact the individual or his organization at a later time in the event that review of your interview notes suggests additional questions. It is often appropriate to ask the individual if there are other persons that he feels you should contact on this subject.

EVALUATION. The last thing that you want is to rush out of one interview and directly into another interview. If you do that, at the end of the day it will be very difficult to remember who said what about anything. Immediately after the interview, go quickly to some quiet spot—conference room or the like—and sit down and review your interview notes carefully. Use a different colored pen or a pencil to add additional detail to the notes that you have just taken. This will allow you to fill in the flavor that was omitted when you recorded just nouns and verbs during the interview. Write as clearly as you can since the interview notes form a permanent source document for your project. Many organizations, such as public accounting firms, use interview note pads made of high rag content bond paper. This paper is more durable than typical note pads and provides a longer lasting permanent record.

During your review of your notes, carefully separate and indicate the interviewee's statements from any impressions that you may have recorded during the interview period. The sample interview note sheet seen in Exhibit 5.2 provides a right margin so that the interviewer can more easily put his impressions in a portion of the interview note pad set aside for that purpose.

Be sure to date and initial every page of your interview notes.

If you interviewed an individual in some association that was not your client, it probably is appropriate to send a thank you letter if the interviewee tried to be helpful. If you were conducting 100 interviews in one organization, sending a thank you letter to each interviewee may be unproductive.

Telephone Surveys

Many of the techniques of personal interviewing apply to telephone interviewing. Telephone interviews include a range from informal data collection by telephone to structured collection programs for nationwide samples. The steps listed in Exhibit 5.1, page 2 are basic actions and coincide with the approaches discussed for personal interviews. The steps are:

- Confirm data to be collected.
- Select target group.
- Select sampling technique.
- Develop sample.
- Prepare survey guide.
- Establish survey approach.
- Conduct survey.
- Accumulate survey guides.

Telephone interviews have gained wide acceptance as a data collection tool in the United States, which has a high quality, widely available telephone network.

The telephone interviews required on a management consulting project frequently are less formal than those required for a project such as a national marketing research survey. The informal telephone interview should receive planning similar to the personal interview. A telephone interview guide should be prepared using the guidelines discussed for personal interviews.

The flow of the telephone interview will also be similar to a personal interview. The planned length usually should be shorter than a personal interview since it is fairly easy to call back later for additional data desired. There are many guides to the length of telephone interviews, but 15 or 20 minutes seems to be an effective upper limit for the busy interviewees usually contacted by management consultants.

The notes from a telephone interview should be handled in a manner similar to personal interview notes. The telephone notes may be more complete since the interviewer does not have to maintain eye contact and can look at what is being written.

Mail Surveys

Mail surveys are an effective data collection technique when used in the appropriate circumstances. The mail survey requires very careful planning and testing. The survey will be guided by the same requirements that guide a personal interview or a telephone survey—the need to answer key questions.

The steps listed in Exhibit 5.2, page 2, are quite basic to mail surveys. The steps are:

- Confirm data to be collected.
- Select target groups.
- Select sampling technique.
- Develop sample.
- Prepare survey instrument.
- Test survey instrument.
- Evaluate and revise instrument.
- Conduct survey.
- Accumulate survey guides.

The successful implementation of a mail survey is an art. Different consultants may use different approaches with equally good, or bad, results. The details of conducting a mail survey are described in several references listed in the bibliography (especially see Dillman, 1978).

3.2. Observe the Activity of People and Systems

For many types of studies it is necessary to have accurate and detailed information regarding the actual operations that take place in a particular work unit. In those circumstances, it often is necessary to have a member of the project team observe the work situation and time, count, measure, or otherwise document the production process. Typically, the following steps would accomplish the observation.

Develop Observation Worksheets

The observation worksheets would be developed to respond directly to the key questions identified during the planning stage. The team member assigned to perform the observation would develop an approach to the actual observation and to the format of the worksheet. This approach and the structure of the observation worksheet would typically be reviewed with the project manager to determine if additional items should be collected or if some items on the worksheet may be best covered by someone else on the project team. The worksheet would include data elements such as the following:

- Organization observed.
- Work unit.

- Location.
- Period covered.
- Sampling rate.
- Hours sampled.
- Identification of individuals or processes sampled.
- Types of operation.
- Name of the observer.

A typical observation worksheet format is presented in Exhibit 5.3.

Coordinate Observations and Obtain Approvals

It is particularly important for observation of people that the purpose, type of observation, units to be observed, and times of observation are carefully coordinated with a principal client and other management and supervisory officials in the organization to be observed. Such observations can generate a substantial amount of concern and resistance on the part of individual employees and labor unions if the observations are not carefully justified to each level of management.

Explain the Process Carefully to the Workers to be Observed

Before the observations begin, it is important to explain carefully to the individuals included in the work unit to be observed the purpose of the observation and exactly what the observer will be doing and recording during the course of the observation. It is sometimes very important to ensure that there is a clear understanding on the part of the workers regarding those things that will not be observed and recorded.

Observe the Activity

The actual observations of such operations as industrial processes, office activity, and data processing center operation are quite diverse in the techniques employed and the data desired. Refer to the bibliography for specific information sources regarding work sampling and other techniques for actually collecting the data. Exhibit 5.3 is a typical observation worksheet for an industrial process.

Complete the Worksheet

Before the observer leaves the work station, a careful check should be made to be sure that the worksheet is complete and legible, and is dated, timed, and

EXHIBIT 5.3   Observation of Activity Worksheet

Organization	Work Center	Period Sample D	Observer
Location	Function	Sampling Rate	Date

	Sampled Entity or Activity								
	Period								

signed by the observer. These worksheets would then be included in the project file in the workpaper structure dictated by the outline of the final report.

3.3. Review Reports and Documents

The collection of information from existing published and unpublished documents is a major source of data for most projects. Since there is such an abundance of material available on most all subjects, it is very important to approach this review process in an efficient manner. This section presents some suggestions for obtaining relevant data from the written record that other people have made of their activities.

Develop a Document Review Worksheet

A worksheet is very useful because it assists in focusing the research on those subjects that are of specific interest to the project. It provides a guideline to measure what has been accomplished and to determine when the details collected have reached an appropriate level. Exhibit 5.4 is an example of a documentation review worksheet.

The review worksheet can be useful for communicating with new staff members and can serve as a reminder to initiate the appropriate action early in the fact collection period.

Conduct a Literature Search

Some review of the available literature may have been made during the planning phase, but at this time a thorough literature search should be made using an updated list of key words and phrases developed during the project. It is usually effective to enlist the services of your company's librarian, a librarian in a public library, or a commercial search service. The National Technical Information Service in the U.S. Department of Commerce has indexed references on many subjects and will perform special searches.

Obtain the Documents

Obtaining relevant documents from the client organization or related project reports from similar organizations can sometimes best be performed by the project team. Usually, obtaining documents from public or private libraries or other reference sources can be more efficiently performed by a librarian if you plan your project well enough to allow several days lead time to permit the

EXHIBIT 5.4 Documentation Review Worksheet

I T E M N O	Key Question and Key Words	SEARCH TYPE				
		Client Library	Office Library	Assigned To Librarian	Requested of_____ Service	Other ?_____
					Prepared By Date Reviewed By Date	Page ____ Of ____

professional librarians to obtain the material for you. If you plan properly, you frequently can identify the materials required in sufficient time to permit the items to be mailed or picked up by support staff. If you wait until the last minute, valuable professional staff time may be used to scurry around looking for documents.

Review the Documents

Once you have the documents in hand, it is useful to set up a structure for efficiently reviewing a number of documents rather than laboriously studying a small percentage of the documents that you obtained. There are several guidelines for review of books or formal reports. These guidelines include reviewing the background of the author or the organization that conducted the study or wrote the book. The background of the author(s) or organizations sometimes gives you an insight into how to prioritize your time in looking at the documents you have. After the review of the author to determine whether that author might have something to contribute on your subject, scan the table of contents to determine if the flow of the document is such that it is likely to contribute to your needs. If the contents flow to your liking, read the introduction quickly to try to determine the flavor of the book and again decide if it meets your needs. If, again, the answer is positive, then quickly skim the book to get an understanding of the types of subheadings and the substance of the chapters. This skim, in many cases, will permit you to zero in on the section of the document that has the data that may prove to be useful to your specific collection purposes. In some cases, you'll be able to refer to an index that will direct you to the page or pages containing the specific topic in which you are interested.

Complete Review Worksheets

The culmination of the document review process is to transfer those key bits of data out of the documents that you review and onto a workshseet where they may be used and integrated into the project data base. As with the other worksheets described previously in this chapter, much emphasis should be placed on developing an audit trail at the time of the preparation of the worksheet. Each entry on the worksheet would list at least a page number of the source document and the full identification of the source document would be clearly indicated in the worksheets. Sometimes it is critical to have the revision number or issue date of the document that you are reviewing. The reviewer should also initial and date each page of the workpapers as they are developed. Exhibit 5.5 is an example of a documentation review workpaper.

EXHIBIT 5.5   Documentation Review Workpaper

Document Reviewed		Publ. Date	
Author	Publisher	Revision	
Where Document Obtained			

Page No.	EXTRACTED FACTS		
		Prepared By Date	Page ____
		Prepared By Date	Of ____

3.4. Test Procedures and Practices

An important aspect of many projects is to determine if a particular system or procedure is actually working in accordance with its statutory, advertised, or regulated standards. Thus it is often appropriate to conduct a review of the performance of a system or a procedure to determine whether the system provides the results that are indicated in formal documentation or required procedures. The following typical steps may be used to test the procedures.

Develop Testing Worksheets

The development of this worksheet encourages the definition of the testing procedure to be focused strictly on the questions identified during the planning stage of the project. This permits a clear focus on what should be tested and what is not relevant for this particular project. The testing worksheet will include the questions that require an answer, the basic parameters of interest in the test, and an indication of the standards to be used to judge the performance.

Select the Practices and Procedures for Systems to be Tested

The selection of the actual systems or procedures to be tested will often require a preliminary survey of the client organization if this has not been accomplished already during the planning phase. For instance, if it were appropriate for your project, you might select an automated system to consolidate a day's receipts from 40 off-track betting offices as a topic for undergoing a controlled test. In a manufacturing organization, an automated or manual inventory control system may be selected to be tested to determine if its many input and output functions really operate in the way that is formally prescribed.

Coordinate and Obtain Approval of the Test

It is important to discuss with the host organization the purpose of the test that you wish to conduct, the conditions of the test, the duration of the test, and the resources you will need from the host organization to be able to conduct this kind of test. It's also important to get the support or concurrence of key management and operations personnel. If you conduct a test of a particular system and then base some portion of your conclusions or recommendations on the results of this test, and there was a very simple operational step you were not aware of and thus did not incorporate into your test procedure, causing your results to be invalid, your entire project can be placed in jeopardy of having a loss of credibility.

Obtain Detailed Data about the Procedure

It is incumbent on the project staff to obtain a detailed operating procedure for the system or practice to be tested. Usually a major test of the system is to determine whether the system is actually performing in accordance with its published documentation. These procedures may be found in directives, manufacturers manuals, or other files in the organization.

Develop or Select Input Data for the Test

In many cases it is appropriate for the project team to develop a dummy set of data they can check independently to insert in the established system or procedure to be able to measure the results of the system on the hypothetical data base. These dummy data could be (1) selected values for inventory levels at each storage location of an inventory control system for which the project team has already calculated what the totals should be, (2) revenue and expense entries for each location of a financial reporting system for a company with distributed outlets that are all profit centers, or (3) a set of a day's transactions for a financial institution with a high volume of high-value transactions that necessitates daily reconciliation.

Establish Controls for the Test

Frequently it is necessary for the project team to establish the type of controls that will be required for the test. This can include access to the system during the time of the test, security of the system or physical surroundings during the test period, or the selection of other performance periods of the system against which to measure the results of the test period.

Conduct the Test

The actual conduct of the test will vary substantially depending on the nature of the system or procedure to be tested. The techniques of the actual test would be guided by the technology involved in data processing, industrial engineering, auditing, and so on.

Evaluate the Results

The results of the tests may be evaluated against published specifications describing expected system performance. For example, manual calculations may be performed for an automated process to determine if the results can be duplicated. The results may be weighed against other performance measures that are relevant to the project issues, or they could be measured against the questions developed for the topic in the study. This type of review would likely continue into the analysis phase described in Chapter 6.

Complete the Test Worksheets

The worksheets from any particular test would include calculation sheets, data processing runs, and notes made during the actual test period. These would be reviewed carefully by the project team and each page containing handwritten information would be dated and signed by a member of the project team.

3.5. Advantages and Disadvantages

The four methods for fact collection just described have individual strengths and weaknesses.

Interviews are an effective method of collecting judgments and predictions of, or plans for, future activity. They also are useful for identifying new topics to investigate and permit interactive discussions between the interviewee and the consultant. The major drawbacks to interviews are that they are time consuming and expensive.

Telephone interviews are efficient to conduct from a central location and a high completion rate can be achieved using frequent callbacks. Since the survey may be conducted from a central location, better supervision can be achieved and thus less experienced interviewers may be used. The principal disadvantages are the inability to observe the interviewee in his or her surroundings, the limited ability to establish rapport, and the need for simple questions.

Mail surveys are useful when very broad coverage (including international) and a large volume of responses are needed. The major disadvantages include low completion rates, the need for high quality lists, the unreliability of the mail, the difficulty in following up, and the lack of knowledge about who actually answered the questionnaire.

The review of documentation generally provides less timely data than the other three methods but can be an effective method of establishing a baseline of prior work on the subject.

Observation of activity can provide accurate, documented data regarding the existing situation. They must be handled carefully to minimize the negative feelings from those who are being observed.

Tests of procedure are often the only method to determine if a system or process performs as it is supposed to. The tests require much care to set up and may also be expensive to conduct.

The uses, advantages, and disadvantages of each of the four methods of fact collection are presented in Exhibit 5.6.

4. DEVELOPING FINDINGS

After the collection of data by one or more of the four methods described in the previous paragraphs, the next step is to develop findings. As indicated in Chapter 2, findings are simple, nonjudgmental sentences that answer a key question and provide further direction to the subject under study.

Each of the key questions identified during the planning stage would be reviewed to determine if that question is still relevant and a finding is still required. For those key questions that require findings, the use of a findings worksheet (Exhibit 5.7) is a helpful technique. The findings worksheet allows project staff to focus on the exact question being addressed. A specific data element will be transferred from the interview notes or other data collection work papers to the findings worksheet to which it contributes. That element may appear on numerous findings worksheets. Most of the data collected will not be transferred to findings worksheets since they are relevant to the subject under study but not specifically required to answer any key question. This process of selecting the specific bits of data that will help answer each key question provides a substantial contribution to reducing the data base to a manageable size. Each data element transferred will have the page number, and sometimes the paragraph number, of the fact collection worksheet from which it was obtained.

One useful technique in developing a finding is to circle or underline those important words included in the transferred facts and then link these words together to form a finding. Thus a finding should consist principally of the words used by the interviewees or appearing in the source documents. These findings worksheets may be used as an information sharing technique among the project team and for communicating the status of a project to the project manager.

5. CASE STUDY

After receipt of approval of the work plan from the firm management and from his client, Bill's next step was to begin the data collection process in accordance

EXHIBIT 5.6   Fact Collection Considerations

Collection Processes	Usually Used to Collect	Advantages	Disadvantages
Observe people's responses			
Interviews	Judgments Data Other contract points Other questions to be answered	Flexible Fuller understanding of data Allows preselling of study results	Time consuming Expensive
Telephone Surveys	Data Preferences	Efficient Broad geographic coverage High completion rates	Cannot observe interviewee Needs simple questions
Mail Surveys	Large quantities of structured data	Very broad coverage High quantity	Low completion rates Requires high-quality lists
Reviews of Documentation	Relevant published data	May cover broad scopes Efficient	Difficult to obtain "feel" for data
Observations of Activity	Data on work flow Time and motion information	Measures actual activity rather than official procedures	Can generate strong negative feelings from client's staff
Tests of Procedures	Data on parameters of computer programs Inputs and outputs of control systems	Positive verification of procedure accuracy	Requires careful coordination with client's staff

with the work plan. To establish good communications among the many organizations involved in a multijurisdiction, multidiscipline study such as this, the development of committees in each of the disciplines was encouraged and achieved. These committees, and the individual members, provided valuable information about the status and feelings of the public safety agencies in the area and provided helpful assistance in determining what officials needed to be interviewed and in coordinating these interviews.

EXHIBIT 5.7   Findings Worksheet

DESCRIPTION OF TASK _____

_____

WHAT KEY QUESTION IS BEING ANALYZED?_____
(Each task may have multiple questions)

_____

_____

WHAT RELEVANT FACTS HAVE YOU COLLECTED WHICH WILL HELP ANSWER THE KEY QUESTION?

WORK PAPERS
PAGE NUMBER   RESTATEMENT OF RECORDED FACT

_____   _____

_____   _____

_____   _____

_____   _____

_____   _____

_____   _____

_____   _____

_____   _____

_____   _____

_____   _____

_____   _____

_____   _____

WHAT FINDING(S) MAY BE DRAWN FROM THE FACTS LISTED ABOVE?

_____

_____

_____

_____

	PREPARED BY DATE	PAGE No. _____
	REVIEWED BY DATE	OF _____

One member of the project team conducted a literature search to find out what other people may have done on this subject. Another of the project team members collected, through interviews and from special computer printouts, the data required for an analysis of crime intensity by geographic area that the transit system passes through.

One data collection task that Bill conducted himself was to identify related projects throughout the country and to contact appropriate management officials or consultants of related projects around the country. Frank discussions of the strengths and weaknesses of earlier related projects can benefit almost any project.

The team then fanned out among the community to conduct a carefully planned and carefully worded series of interviews with officials of the:

- Transit organization.
- Police departments.
- Fire departments.
- Rescue departments.
- Legal organizations.
- Community organizations and other officials.

After data collection was completed, each team member concentrated on completing findings worksheets for the questions relating to his or her topic of responsibility. The completion of the findings worksheets required a considerable amount of discussion among the team members and sharing of relevant facts. An example of a findings worksheet is presented in Exhibit 5.8.

A meeting of the project team is held and all of the major findings worksheets are presented and discussed. Many of the findings are acceptable to the project team and are included in the group that requires no further data collection. However, there are several findings that the group has some concern about and follow-up data collection is scheduled. Near the end of the meeting, Bill, the project manager, presents the findings worksheets to the vice president to provide him hands-on data to indicate the status of the project.

After these discussions, Bill assembles the findings into a findings summary sheet, organized by chapter and subchapter of the final report outline.

6. SUMMARY

The purpose of fact collection is to collect enough facts to answer the key questions.

EXHIBIT 5.8   Findings Worksheet

DESCRIPTION OF TASK ___7 – PERFORM   FEASIBILITY ANALYSIS___

WHAT KEY QUESTION IS BEING ANALYZED? _What are the key issues_
(Each task may have multiple questions)
involved in developing a security system for a
transit organization?

WHAT RELEVANT FACTS HAVE YOU COLLECTED WHICH WILL HELP ANSWER THE KEY QUESTION?

WORK PAPERS PAGE NUMBER	RESTATEMENT OF RECORDED FACT
I/E/pg.47	• the (public) must have (confidence) in the system
I/S/pg.54	• the fire, police, and rescue services must provide (better cooperation) among themselves
I/R/pg.3	• (new legislation) will be required for an effective system.
I/S/pg.20	• the new (system) must have a low enough (cost) that the local govern- ment will support it
I/E/pg.15	• must be configured in such a way that (management control) can be exerted over the entire system

WHAT FINDING(S) MAY BE DRAWN FROM THE FACTS LISTED ABOVE?

The key issues involved in developing a security system are public confidence, new legislation, system cost, better agency cooperation, and management control.

PREPARED BY BFK	PAGE No. _1_
DATE 10 Mar, 80	
REVIEWED BY £7K	OF _1_
DATE 20 Mar 80	

The four basic fact collection techniques are:

- Obtain people's responses.
- Observe the activity of people and systems.
- Review written documentation.
- Test working procedures.

People's responses can be obtained by:

- Personal interviews.
- Telephone surveys.
- Mail surveys.

The five stages of an interview are generally defined as:

- Planning.
- Opening.
- Asking core questions.
- Closing.
- Evaluating.

Findings are simple nonjudgmental sentences which answer a key question and provide further direction to the subject under study.

CHAPTER SIX
Analyzing the Situation

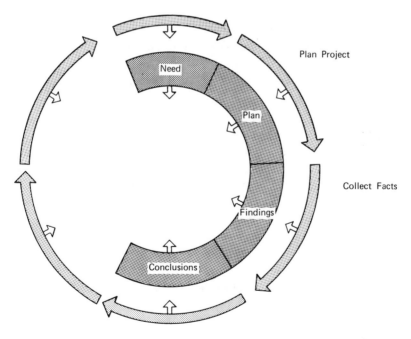

Identify Need

Plan Project

Collect Facts

Analyze Data

Need

Plan

Findings

Conclusions

A nalysis means different things to different people. Charlie Chan on the late show exhibits one form of analysis by applying much intuition in solving a complex criminal case. That type of analysis, however, is not well suited to the conduct of a management consulting project. The intent of this chapter is to provide a framework for a more logical approach to the analysis phase of problem solving.

1. PURPOSE OF ANALYSIS

The purpose of analysis for a project is to:

- Break the problem down into its constituent elements.
- Develop conclusions at an appropriate level of detail for the problem under study.

Breaking down a problem into its constituent elements may be done a number of ways depending on the type of project under study. For example, for a work measurement project the analysis would require that the organization be divided into its subunits, those subunits divided into work units, and possibly those work units into particular work processes. When facts about the particular work processes are collected and arrayed in that fashion, the problem has been broken down from consideration of workload factors on the organizational level to consideration of workload factors at the work process level in the work unit.

Once the data have been broken into the appropriate level of detail, then conclusions normally must be drawn regarding the meaning of that set of facts. For example, for a data processing survey, it may not be particularly useful to reach a conclusion saying the data processing center does not work well. It may be appropriate to reach conclusions regarding the amount of delay time being encountered by remote users trying to access the data center, about the percentage utilization of the CPU, or the number of job reruns necessary as the result of operator mistakes in the data center.

2. WHAT IS ANALYSIS?

Analysis may be defined as separation of a material or abstract entity into constituent parts or elements. Analysis, as described in this chapter, is a process for the orderly selection and use of analytical techniques for breaking down the situation under study into its basic elements. As discussed earlier, all of the analysis in the project does not occur during the "analysis phase." Analysis, in one form or another, is involved in almost every phase of any project. The analysis in this phase is in particular those formal steps that one takes, and should document, to move from the basic findings described in the previous chapter to conclusions about those findings.

3. PROCESS OF ANALYSIS

The actions described in this section provide a generalized step-by-step procedure for sorting your facts into their constituent elements so that conclusions may be drawn. Analysis begins at the proposal stage, or the problem definition stage, in the identification and categorization of issues to be resolved during the study. Additional analysis is performed during the planning phase when the report outline is developed and key questions are developed for that outline. This analysis further divides the basic issues into the categories that will be developed and described in the final report. In Exhibit 6.1 the relationships among the analysis activities involved in the project are depicted.

Additional analysis is performed during the fact collection phase when the findings and supporting data are developed and organized in the manner that will be used in the final report. There is additional analysis at this point on the part of the project team in the selection of relevant facts to be used to draw the findings and in the selection of the major findings that will be transferred into the report. These actions are the preliminary tasks which are available when one begins the formal phase we call analysis.

The three basic activities performed during the analysis phase are to classify, to question, and to compare. These three activities are applied through a very wide variety of specific analytical techniques used, depending on the nature of the problem and the skills of the consultants. These techniques are generally divided into *qualitative* and *quantitative* techniques.

The results of the application of all of the techniques used in analysis are *conclusions*.

Another way to describe the analysis process is to look at the sequential steps that one would go through to analyze a problem. The steps below are described in a sequential process, but one must remember that the analysis process is an interative activity that begins in the proposal stage and includes more comprehensive cycles as it comes through planning and data collection. The following generalized steps provide a framework for analysis.

EXHIBIT 6.1   Process of Analysis

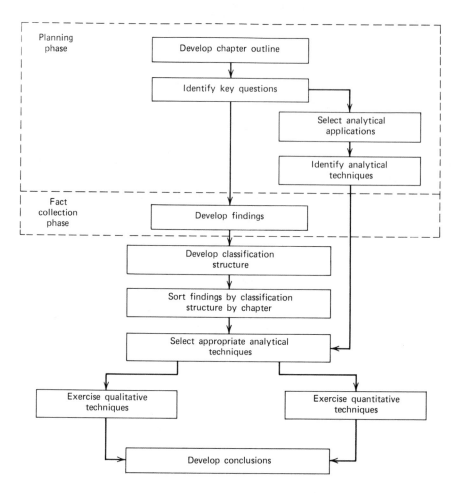

3.1.   Develop a Classification Structure

The classification structure, into which the facts, findings, and other relevant information will be categorized, are confirmed, or selected, at this point. This categorization will take place based on the most appropriate parameters of this project. The basis for classification could include such structures as:

- Physical shapes.
- Functions.

- Uses.
- Funding sources.
- Physical composition of the elements involved.
- Organizational relationships.

An example of the use of physical shapes as a basis for classification might be for a document-handling study where the products to be handled were sorted by:

- Flats, regular size.
- Flats, oversize.
- Boxes, less than 6 inches in the largest dimension.
- Boxes, more than 6 inches in the largest dimension.
- Cylindrical, larger than 6 inches.

Functions might be used as a way to categorize the data in a police management study where the activities were categorized as:

- Management.
- Administration.
- Preventive patrol.
- Investigation.
- Community relations.

Categorization by uses might take place in a market research study by listing the end use consumers as:

- Industrial.
- Commercial.
- Residential.
- Recreational.

Funding sources might be used in an organization study to categorize the methods used to support the various organizational units. This might include:

- Appropriated yearly funds.
- Appropriated multiyear funds.

- Appropriated no-year funds.
- Nonappropriated funds such as donated funds or enterprise funds.

An example of categorization by physical composition would be a product design study where the performance of the planned product would be evaluated based on manufacture out of:

- Steel.
- Aluminum.
- Plastic.
- Ceramic.

Organizational relationships might be used to categorize the data in a work methods and procedures study as follows:

- Division A:
    - Branch 1.
    - Branch 2.
- Division B:
    - Branch 3.
    - Branch 4.
- Division C:
    - Branch 5.
    - Branch 6.

The classification structure may be a subset of the structure chosen for the report outline.

3.2. Sort the Findings by Category

This step consists of reviewing all the relevant findings, data, or other appropriate information and sorting and arranging this information by the chosen classification structure.

The physical categorization could be made using a series of file folders to segregate the information based on the chosen structure, a three-ring notebook divided by the appropriate structure titles, or a series of index cards, which could be easily shuffled and rearranged.

For projects that include the use of data processing techniques it may be easy to get the data sorted into the appropriate categories if the required output categories are determined before the data are collected and entered and the software is acquired or developed.

For data collected manually, the preliminary sorting may be performed effectively if the task breakout for the data collection effort is aligned in accordance with the way the data are desired. Then the workpaper binders for the subtask may be a logical component of the data base.

3.3. Select Analytical Techniques

In most projects at this stage, the data obtained would receive a final examination to determine whether the analytical techniques that had been selected and planned are still the most relevant or if changes or modifications should be made.

There are numerous analytical techniques that can be applied to modern problem solving projects. The two basic categories are qualitative techniques and quantitative techniques.

QUALITATIVE ANALYSIS

Qualitative analysis is defined as breaking down, in descriptive or judgmental terms, those things that cannot be measured precisely with a numerical scale. Some of the more commonly used types of qualitative analysis techniques are the following.

Basic Question. This technique consists of taking a particular topic under study and proceeding to break it down by asking a series of basic questions. Examples of this could be:

- What does this mean?
- What are the elements in this box?
- How is it manufactured?
- How many pieces are in this product?
- Who authorizes expenditures in this organization?
- How are expenditure levels monitored?
- How often are expenditures levels monitored?
- Who monitors the expenditures?
- What documents are used to monitor the expenditures?

Pattern Search. The essence of this technique is to review major activities involved for the subclassification of information to look for patterns along the various functions or activities. An example of a pattern search would be for a security officer for a large manufacturing firm to sift and sort the reports on thefts until a pattern was noticed. He may observe that a large percentage of thefts took place ten or more days after the company payday and a very low percentage occurred within five days after payday. Additional analysis might indicate that a high percentage of thefts took place on dark moonless nights.

Attribute Listing. This technique consists of developing categories for the subject under study, developing descriptors by these categories, then expanding the descriptors. This would include categories such as physical (shape, weight, length, etc.), economic (cost, revenues, etc.), and social (informal groupings, accepted practices, unaccepted practices).

For an information system detailed design project it may be useful to use an attribute listing technique to analyze the requirements for input/output terminals. This might be:

- Physical:
  - Desktop.
  - Weight less than 35 pounds.
  - One-piece construction.
  - Choice of three colors.
- Operation:
  - Minimum training required to operate.
  - No programming background necessary for operators.
  - Full alphanumeric keyboard and video display.
  - Hard copy printout included.
- Performance:
  - Minimum MTBF 2000 hours.
  - Internal modem for interface over unconditioned telephone lines.
  - Electrical interface per EIA Standard RS 232 C.
- Cost:
  - Acquisition cost.
  - Annual maintenance cost.

During equipment tradeoff analysis these attribute descriptors could be expanded for each alternative to be analyzed.

Forced Relationships. This technique consists of forcing comparisons between different elements of the situation under study to determine the common characteristics and differences. In a management study of a large manufacturing company, one might ask:

- How is Division A, which is not profitable, different from Division B, which is highly profitable?
- What characteristics of Division A are similar to Division B?
- What characteristics of Division A are different from the characterstics of its principal competitor?

Matrix Method. The matrix method is one of the most commonly used techniques of analysis. It consists of developing a chart, or matrix, of one set of variables versus other characteristics of the problem under study. A matrix analysis might include basic elements of the problem under study arrayed against such factors as performance and costs.

For an analysis of alternative systems for long-distance telephone service available to a small company, a matrix such as the accompanying one might be useful. This matrix has both qualitative and quantitative data.

Alternative Long-Distance Service	Circuit Quality	System Reliability	Access Delay	Dialing Time (seconds)
A	Good	High	Short	10
B	Good	High	Queue during peak hours	15
C	Good	Medium	Short	20
D	Good	High	Long	20
E	Fair	High	Short	20

Reference Projections. To obtain a better understanding of a system or a process, a reference projection is sometimes helpful. A reference projection (Ackoff, 1978) is an extrapolation of the existing situation into the future with the use of assumptions known to be false. Thus situations may be identified that cause all parties to agree that something must be changed. The situations may also suggest topics or directions for change.

If a reference projection had been made in 1970 regarding the growth of the number, size, and use of automobiles in the United States for a 40-year period, the total annual gasoline consumption by automobiles in the United States in the year 2010 might have been in excess of the projected world's supply by that time. That type of projection would have suggested or demanded that transportation and other energy-related policies be reviewed.

Visualize Others. This technique frequently is used when the analyst feels somewhat stymied by the problem. It consists of sitting back and reflecting on the topic you are analyzing and asking yourself how someone else might approach this particular problem. If it were a political problem, one might ask how Franklin D. Roosevelt would have approached it. If it were a humanitarian venture, one might ask how Albert Schweitzer would have approached the situation. For a legal problem, one might ask how Oliver Wendell Holmes would have approached it.

Ask People Not Involved in Project. It may be helpful to ask a person who has no connection with the project about how it should be broken down. You may ask another person in your field of specialization or you may ask someone in a totally unrelated field.

If you were performing an urban planning study and were trying to structure an analysis of factors that influence urban growth, you might contact an anthropologist, a historian, or an engineer and ask how each would structure the analysis. It is possible that you would elicit some concepts that had not been considered previously.

QUANTITATIVE ANALYSIS

Quantitative analysis techniques are used when you can count or measure the quantity being examined. In other words, you have numerical information to work with. Some techniques are designed to assist the analyst to operate directly on the data from the system being studied. These techniques include certain cost analysis and statistical procedures. The cost analysis techniques include:

- Breakeven analysis.
- Incremental cost analysis.
- Opportunity cost analysis.
- Economic life.
- Return on investment.

- Present value.
- Cost benefit analysis.

Other techniques assist the analyst to construct a representation of reality (a model) that will simulate the real situation. Any model used should be structured to reflect the specific questions that need to be answered for the project. If a model is built, it should be developed only to the level of detail required to answer the questions under consideration. Since the model is a representation of reality, and thus is approximate and incomplete, the analyst should be cautious in applying the outputs from the model.

If a model describes facts and the relationships among them, and includes no value system, it is descriptive. If it contains a value system, it is a prescriptive (or normative) model representing what things might or ought to be.

Models can be described by various characteristics. One way to define these characteristics is as follows:

- Use:
    - Descriptive.
    - Prescriptive.
- Source data:
    - Empirical.
    - Theoretical.
- Complexity:
    - Linear.
    - Nonlinear.
- Predictability:
    - Deterministic.
    - Probabilistic.
- Change interval:
    - Discrete.
    - Continuous.
- Time base:
    - Static.
    - Dynamic.

Most modeling techniques are used to predict the association among variables. Many of these measures of association are based on regression or correlation techniques. The consultant should be cautious in inferring a causal relationship when it may be only association that has been demonstrated.

To assist the consultant in determining the types of analytical techniques available, a structured list has been developed. A practicing operations researcher may not agree with some of the categorizations but I hope the presentation is useful to most readers. The quantitative models have been divided into deterministic, stochastic, and those that generally are for time series data.

- Deterministic models:
  - Graph theory.
  - Linear programming.
  - Networks.
  - Integer programming.
  - Nonlinear programming.
- Stochastic models:
  - Queuing theory.
  - Value/utility theory.
  - Decision analysis.
  - Inventory control.
  - Game theory.
  - Search theory.
  - Simulation theory.
  - Dynamic programming.
- Regression analysis:
  - Simple regression.
  - Multiple regression.
  - Econometric models.
- Time series analysis:
  - Smoothing.
  - Decomposition.
- Time series analysis (autoregressive/moving average, ARMA):
  - Box Jenkins.
  - Multivariate time series.

Many statistical techniques are included in the analytical models listed above. A basic list of commonly used statistical techniques in consulting projects is as follows:

- Descriptive techniques:
    - Parametric tests (such as F, t, Chi-square).
    - Nonparametric (such as rank order).
- Correspondence techniques:
    - Correlation.
    - Regression.

Several excellent reference texts in operations research, forecasting, and statistics are listed in the bibliography.

After the analysis techniques are selected and completed, there are many approaches to presenting the results. These presentation techniques include:

- Graphic:
    - Continuous distribution (straight line, curve).
    - Discontinuous distribution (bar, band, step function).
    - Noncontiguous (pie chart).
    - Flow diagram (PERT, CPM).
    - Special format (area diagram, map).
- Tabular:
    - Frequency distributions.
    - Ratio/percentage distribution.

There are many types of analytical technique available. Much care must be exercised in selecting the techniques to use for any project. It has been said that the selection of the techniques to use is more important than the actual execution of the technique.

Additional definition of many of the techniques discussed above is included in the appendix.

3.4. Develop Conclusions

Analysis consists of breaking the subject down into its constituent elements to permit more detailed examination. Conclusions are the judgment of the consultant regarding the meaning of the findings. The development of conclusions generally is based on the relationships among the variables considered. The analyst should use caution at this point since the relationships among the various factors may be difficult to understand.

Variables that change together, positively or negatively, are said to be *associ-*

ated, and there *may* be a causal relationship between the two. A causal relationship exists only if a change in variable A causes a predictable direction of change in variable B.

If no association can be established between two variables, it can be concluded that no causal relationship exists under those circumstances. If the situation changes, the conclusion is invalid and must be proved again.

Some of the more common difficulties in problem solving arise when quantitative techniques are used and the client, and sometimes the consultant, fails to remember that correlation and regression analysis are measures of association and do not define causality. Thus the quantitative techniques are useful tools but the results must be used by carefully applying the judgment of the consultant and possibly others.

4. DISCUSSION

The preceding summary of some of the most commonly accepted analytical techniques indicates the many different approaches that can be taken to analyze projects. A more general approach to the analysis phase might be obtained by reviewing a list of questions about the analysis process itself. Some of these questions are:

- What are the major issues involved in this subject we are studying?
- What are the most relevant questions we have asked and now have answers to?
- What are the links among the key questions and findings that we now have?
- What types of conclusion are needed to be able to continue with the subject under study?
- What data and findings have been developed to this point and are they appropriate for developing the types of conclusions mentioned above?
- What analytical techniques must be applied to the data or findings to be able to reach the conclusions needed?
- How do you select among the various possible alternative techniques those that could be applied to the problem?

An approach to finishing the analysis process is also usable during the synthesis process to be discussed in the next chapter. This process is to look for:

- Basic relationships.
- Motivation of key personnel.

In most situations there are basic relationships between the inputs and the outputs of the situation under study that can be identified. If the problem is to study the feasibility of a cement plant and the country in which the plant is to be built has only one region that produces raw materials for the plant, and access transportation routes are controlled by a competing company, then that is a key relationship with respect to inputs to the plant. If the marketing projections indicate that a substantial percentage of the output of the plant would have to be exported, and a competing political group, or organization, has control over the port facilities, then that is a key relationship.

A key consideration in any problem analysis is to attempt to determine the motivation of the key personnel. Two questions must be asked for each of the key individuals involved:

- What happens for a particular scenario to the interests of each key individual?
- What is it in each individual's best interest to do?

For each scenario of possible outcomes for a situation, if you can postulate what the best interests of each key individual dictates in that situation, you can often get a better understanding of a way the critical elements in the problem should be structured. This type of analysis can influence conclusions substantially in terms of what might be achievable in the next phase, synthesizing alternative solutions.

5. CASE STUDY

After Bill and his project team had collected most of the facts that are needed to support this study, they were prepared to begin their analysis. (Actually, the analysis takes place over a long period of time during the project. As data are acquired they are categorized, filed, etc.)

To reach the conclusions necessary to guide this feasibility study, the analysis tasks that the project team performed included:

- Development of a staffing versus coverage model for manpower deployment.

- Development of a salary cost model.
- Development of a comparative staffing model.
- Development of a geographic crime severity model.
- Comparison of legal requirements in the several jurisdictions.

These and other analyses were performed to enable the project team to better understand and to reach conclusions regarding the many segments of the study. The major conclusions are discussed among the project team at an analysis review meeting and are assembled by chapter and subchapter of the final report along with the previously developed key questions and findings.

Once these draft conclusions are developed, Bill coordinates these with the vice president in charge of this project and subsequently with the client. The nuances of each of the conclusions are reviewed with the client and enough background data are provided so that the client feels comfortable with the conclusions.

The conclusions reached at this stage include such statements as: "The confidence that the public has in their personal safety and comfort when and if they use the system will have a significant impact on system revenues."

6. SUMMARY

Analysis breaks down the problem into its constituent elements.
Analysis is performed during all phases of a project.
The three basic activities of analysis are to:

- Classify.
- Question.
- Compare.

The analytical techniques are usually divided into:

- Qualitative.
- Quantitative.

Conclusions are the judgment of the consultant regarding the meaning of the findings.
Variables that change together are said to be associated.

EXHIBIT 6.2 Analysis

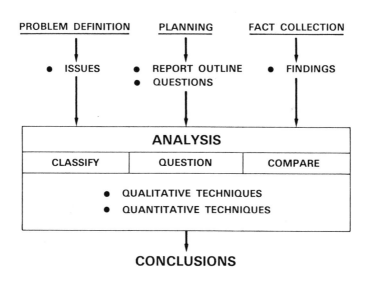

A causal relationship exists only if one variable causes a predictable change in an associated variable.

The consultant should look carefully for:

- Basic relationships.
- Motivation of key personnel.

An overview of the analysis process is depicted in Exhibit 6.2.

CHAPTER SEVEN

Developing
Alternative Solutions

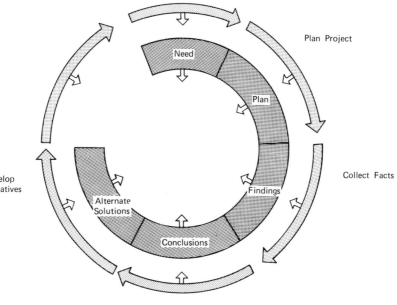

M any of you have been involved in projects where a perfectly reasonable and workable solution was obtained. After such a project was concluded, you might have been asked, "How was the solution developed?" For many projects this is a difficult question to answer because the results seem to develop on an intuitive basis as a result of the familiarity of the project team with the subject as well as their functional skills. This chapter describes a process for logically approaching the identification of alternative solutions and the development of those solutions.

The consultant approaching the development of solutions should consciously review the approaches that might be used to satisfy the client need. Ackoff (1978) has described three ways of dealing with conflict, or developing a course of action for your client.

Solution to a conflict results when one party "wins" over another party. This may involve force. When force is used one or both parties try to remove, eliminate, incapacitate, or inactivate the other party. The fights may be avoided, or terminated, when one party becomes subservient to the other. When fights are halted by outside, stronger parties, the conflict usually will break out again at an intensified level.

Resolution of a conflict is achieved when the parties accept the conditions that created it and compromise on sharing the item in dispute. Negotiation, bargaining, and arbitration are examples of processes to resolve conflicts.

Dissolution of a conflict occurs when the conditions that produced the conflict are removed so the conflict disappears. If two kingdoms are preparing to go to war for control over a bridge, the construction of a second bridge may dissolve the conflict.

The consultant should also be aware that for some types of problems, such as some public policy issues, there may be no "final solutions," but there may be recommended courses of action.

A major part of developing alternative solutions from the information base obtained in Chapter 6 is a process called synthesis. Synthesis is defined as the combining of the constituent elements of separate material or abstract entities into a single or unified entity. Thus for a consulting project, synthesis is the recombination of the various elements of the problem into one or more complete, workable solutions.

1. PURPOSE OF SYNTHESIS

There are two principal purposes to the synthesis phase of a project:

• Develop alternative solutions.
• Document the ideas and alternatives considered.

The development of alternatives normally is necessary to provide a spectrum of possible solutions to the client's need so that the project team can be assured that they have considered an appropriate range of alternatives from which to select a recommendation.

The process of generating ideas and developing these ideas into alternative solutions often is not a carefully documented process. It is important, in my opinion, to document the synthesis process for two reasons. First, by taking a few extra minutes during this synthesis phase to actually record by hand-written notes, memos, and the like, the many ideas and approaches considered, one may stop to examine an idea that may have been summarily dismissed if the thought process was informal and had not been recorded. Second, in the unlikely and unwelcome event that the client will not agree with your conclusions and accept your recommendations, there is added pressure on the thoroughness of your consulting approach and the completeness of your workpapers, or if the extremely unfortunate situation occurs whereby you wind up as a defendent in legal action, you may have to present and justify your workpapers in a court of law.

2. RELATION TO ANALYSIS

As discussed in Chapter 6, analysis is the breaking down of the client's situation into appropriate categories and levels of detail for the information in those categories and the development of conclusions and data regarding these categories. The synthesis phase takes the information and the conclusions available at that elementary level and recombines those elements into complete scenarios or workable alternative solutions to the client's need.

3. THE PROCESS OF SYNTHESIS

Synthesis can take place in a variety of ways for the almost unlimited number of situations that can occur. In this section a generalized process is outlined which can be used as a guide for developing a specific process for any particular project.

Prior to beginning a description of the steps involved, it may be appropriate to briefly discuss some broad questions regarding developing alternative solutions. At the beginning of the synthesis phase it is usually appropriate to ask the following questions:

- What objectives should the alternative solution attempt to fulfill? (This will result principally from a review of the initial statement of need, the issues involved, and from the principal conclusions developed during the analysis phase.)
- What would be your concept of an ideal solution for this situation? (In many cases it is helpful to visualize an ideal, or perfect, solution allowing yourself to be absolutely free of constraints. This thought might shape the range of alternatives you actually develop and carry into final alternatives evaluation.)
- What are the best approaches to developing alternative solutions? (As discussed in Section 3.7 (below), there are several ways to go about identifying alternatives. The consultant should specifically ask and answer this question before getting deeply involved in the synthesis phase.)

A final general consideration, before beginning the actual steps of synthesis, is the question of what types of recommendations are likely to be forthcoming from this project. This includes consideration of the recommendations the client is expecting, and what recommendations may be supported by the data collection and analysis phases. One way to break down the types of recommendations is into the following categories:

- Strategic recommendations.
- Tactical recommendations.
- Task recommendations.

An example of a strategic recommendation would be a recommendation to a company to deemphasize their future reliance on petroleum refining and to place a major emphasis on developing and marketing products in coal liquification or solar energy technology.

An example of a tactical recommendation is if the decision were made to increase concentration on coal production or coal liquification rather than petroleum, a recommendation might be to attempt to take over Consolidated Coal's operations in Southern Indiana or Eastern Coal's operations in Eastern Kentucky.

Examples of task recommendations are: (1) to change the paper flow through the report department, (2) to revise the format of the annual questionnaire, and (3) to add another production line for XYZ product.

We next consider a systematic process for identifying, evaluating, and shaping alternative solutions to client needs. These steps are depicted in Exhibit 7.1.

3.1. Identify the Topics for Solution

The types of solutions that should be developed will be shaped by the conclusions developed during the analysis phase and from the basic issues defined during the need definition phase. In other words, the first step of the process is to be sure to develop a fix on what types of solutions will be developed.

3.2. Organize the Information, Findings, and Conclusions That Relate to the Solutions Needed

After you decide what types of solution will be developed, the next step is to organize the information previously developed and be sure it is in the order that will be appropriate for the types of solutions to be developed. This would also include making another check on the category structure developed during the analysis phase to determine if that structure is appropriate for the building blocks required to put together the solutions that you have now decided that you will build.

3.3. Sort Out Basic Relationships

At this point it will be useful to pause and ask yourself what the basic relationships involved in this process are. What are the inputs, outputs, or major internal actions that are critical to the subject being addressed. For instance, if you were studying the feasibility of building an integrated steel plant in a small country and the rail line from the only source of iron ore came through an adjoining country, then the reliability of the source of iron ore for this feasibility study surely would be a basic relationship.

3.4. Consider the Motivation of Key Personnel

At this point it can be very helpful in ensuring that your alternatives include the correct range of ideas if you consider the motivation of the key people who will be involved in developing or implementing the recommendation. First,

EXHIBIT 7.1 Developing Solutions

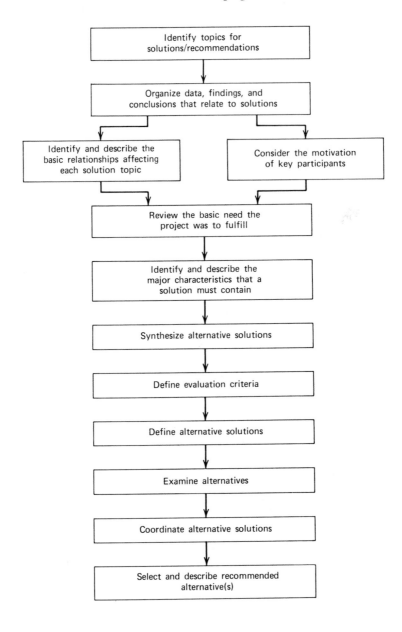

Identify topics for
solutions/recommendations

Organize data, findings, and
conclusions that relate to solutions

Identify and describe the
basic relationships affecting
each solution topic

Consider the motivation
of key participants

Review the basic need the
project was to fulfill

Identify and describe the
major characteristics that a
solution must contain

Synthesize alternative solutions

Define evaluation criteria

Define alternative solutions

Examine alternatives

Coordinate alternative solutions

Select and describe recommended
alternative(s)

you must identify the key personnel who are in place and determine how many must be recruited and hired to implement the recommendation, and then postulate what the motivation of these key people might be. If, for a particular situation, you can hypothesize a range of possible events and then evaluate the likely motivation of the key owners, competitors, and managers, you may find some very useful insights into the way the alternative should be structured. The motivational factors may include such items as:

- Financial rewards.
- Status.
- Promotion.

3.5. Review the Basic Need the Project Was to Fulfill

This step consists of taking the basic issues and the definition of the problem developed in the need identification phase and the conclusions developed in the analysis phase, combined with the basic relationships and key motivation indicated above, and molding these factors into what could be called a revised statement of need. This review and development of the revised statement of need can provide clearer guidelines as to what the alternatives should do.

3.6. Identify and Describe the Major Characteristics
That a Solution Must Contain

The action in this step follows sequentially from 3.5 above in that the basic need to be fulfilled is then described by, among other factors:

- Major elements.
- Personnel requirements.
- Cost.
- Implementation strategy.

In many cases this step will parallel or use a substantial amount of material developed in the analysis phase when the situation was broken down into its constituent elements. The constituent elements (or major factors) will be organized and categorized in the way that makes the most sense for the alternative being considered.

3.7. Synthesize Alternative Solutions

This step, of course, is the heart of the development of alternative solutions. It may also be the most creative part of problem solving, or consulting. It is the time at which you apply the experience, imagination, and judgment of the project team to identify possible new and unique concepts to apply to your client's problems.

The methods that are used to obtain ideas that apply to solving the client's problems are numerous. The methods can be described as structured (morphological), random, or a combination of the two. Some of the more common methods are discussed below.

BRAINSTORMING

Brainstorming probably is one of the most commonly applied techniques used to generate ideas for a solution. Brainstorming may be used at all phases of the problem solving process but is most commonly used for the development of alternatives. It can work well using from two to ten people. Brainstorming is a process of putting a group of people together and applying certain rules to the statements made which maximize the possibility of getting a fast flow of unevaluated ideas in response to a situation. Brainstorming sessions should begin with an open-ended question such as "What are all the solutions possible for situation XXX?"

Alex Osborn, who is generally credited with originating the technique of brainstorming, indicates there are four basic rules for participants:

- Defer judgment (critical analyses of all ideas comes at a later meeting).
- Freewheel (relax and say anything that comes to mind).
- Tag-on (feel free to present a minor variation of a previously discussed idea and go ahead and say it without pausing to evaluate it).
- Quantity is desired (speak up with every relevant, semirelevant, irrelevant and irreverent thought that comes to mind).

The recording of ideas in a brainstorming session should be done in a manner that will not hold up the flow of ideas. It should be accomplished with the use of a stenographer, a tape recorder, or a fast writer on a flip chart or blackboard. The discussion on any particular subject should not run more than 15 minutes. Some people find that another session within a day or two using the same participants is a good technique for eliciting follow-up thoughts.

After all of the basic ideas have been recorded you may convene the same group or a revised group to begin the process of sifting through the ideas to evaluate them.

ASK QUESTIONS

At this point in the study the project team generally is deeply immersed in the details, techniques, and history of the project under study. Sometimes it is useful to ask a simple question of a person not associated with the project. With little or no briefing on the history of the project to date, ask what types of solutions occur to them. Often this method will obtain a very different or unique idea that the project team has not thought of.

SEARCH THE LITERATURE

In many cases it is helpful to perform a literature search to uncover what others have done when confronted with a situation similar to that with which you are working.

DEVELOP AN ANALOGY CHAIN

An analogy chain can be used to stimulate ideas by breaking the subject under consideration into several parameters and then redefining each of the individual parameters. The description of the overall subject can then be changed by linking the parameters back together again using the redefinitions in different groupings. For example, you might happen to be concentrating on the subject of a briefcase. A briefcase is defined by the following parameters and descriptors:

Subject:	Briefcase
Use:	Carry papers
Shape:	Rectangular parallelepiped
Composition:	Leather
Color:	Black

This subject can now be redefined as follows:

Subject:	Tote bag, status symbol, material transporter
Use:	Carry lunch, impress clients, small suitcase
Shape:	Sphere, hemisphere, cube, cylinder
Composition:	Plastic, cloth, paper
Color:	Brown, red, white, etc.

The new alternatives can be obtained by linking the descriptors in various combinations.

SYNECTICS

One technique for generating new ideas has been defined by William J. J. Gordon. His process, Synectics, is a series of techniques that include analogy, metaphor, and simile to develop alternative solutions and fresh points of view. The Synectics process has three stages:

- Stage 1, the examination of the initial situation, analysis of that situation, the identification and description of any preconceptions, and a restatement of the initial situation as a result of this analysis.
- Stage 2, expansion of the limits of your horizon by examining other situations without tying these to the situation that you are now studying, or being concerned about their relationship.
- Stage 3, return to the problem situation with the points of view that you've gained by observing other situations.

Gordon described four paths to creative behavior: (1) detachment and involvement, which means to try to view the problem from the inside as well as the outside environment; (2) deferment, which includes having the patience and the forbearance to accept inputs from any relevant source and to postpone judgments until all available data are in; (3) speculation, which includes developing ideas in an uninhibited manner, developing a wide range of questions, and making a broad range of suppositions; and (4) object autonomy, which means permitting the product (or output) being examined to become the process being experienced.

3.8. Define Evaluation Criteria

The intention of this step is to establish a baseline for the informal and, later, formal measurement of the ideas generated for alternative solutions. The first action is to review the statement of need and develop, from the issues identified, key parameters of any alternative solution. These key parameters can usually be converted to evaluation criteria to judge the potential alternative solutions.

It is often appropriate to consider what type of recommendation is needed. Identification of the general types of recommendations at this stage can often be very useful in determining which ideas are to be discarded and which are to be retained.

The advantages and disadvantages of each alternative solution may be measured by indices for each. The combination of these indices (sometimes in mathematical form) is called a criterion function and provides a rating method for each alternative.

Based on the foregoing considerations, and other considerations that may be unique to that project, develop measures of performance for the alternative solutions. These measures of performance, or standards, can be used to select among the ideas and later be used to formally measure the alternative solutions developed.

3.9. Define Alternative Solutions

This is a key step in providing innovative and responsible solutions to client situations. This step consists of selecting key ideas from among the many that have been generated earlier and requires the consultant to introduce creativity into the problem solving process. This creativity must be tempered with sound judgment to produce a workable solution to the client situation.

The first action involved is usually to classify the many ideas generated during the synthesis step. These ideas may be sorted by organizational unit (if that is the most relevant for the type of recommendation which you are planning to develop), function, or other appropriate category.

The ideas may then be mixed and sorted and sifted in a number of ways. The most commonly used technique for mixing the ideas is simply to mull them over informally to determine whether the consultant can piece together appropriate alternative solutions. This method may also allow significant elements to be overlooked. Other techniques that can be used to mix ideas include developing analogy chains, as described in 3.7 above, or the use of forced relationships as described in the appendix.

After the basic ideas have been sifted and sorted, the most promising ideas need to be pulled forward and given additional review. This review can be a screening based on personal opinion and personal experience or by visualizing the results that might be achieved if a particular idea were carried through to a recommendation and implemented.

A few of the most relevant ideas would then be carried forward and screened for their general relevance and their completeness in responding to the evaluation criteria described above.

Each of the possible alternative solutions would then be described in more detail. The three elements that would be included in the description of each alternative solution are:

- The action required to implement that solution.
- The operation of that solution.
- The configuration of the solution.

A solution to a problem is obtained when a set of conditions is identified for those elements over which the decision maker has control and that, when operated under the defined constraints, will provide satisfactory performance.

3.10. Examine the Alternatives

Each of the alternative solutions that will be reviewed in detail and possibly coordinated with your client will be formally measured against the evaluation criteria developed earlier. Through the use of matrix techniques, performance description techniques, cost analysis, or other appropriate methods for evaluating the expected performance of each alternative solution, the relative performance of each alternative will be developed. This will usually include qualitative and quantitative measurement approaches. The performance characteristics of each alternative solution would then be summarized to facilitate their discussion with client and management personnel.

3.11. Coordinate Alternative Solutions

The selection of the alternative solutions and the evaluation of the principal alternative solutions must be carefully reviewed within the project team, with the management of the consulting organization, and with key client personnel. If the client has been involved during the course of the project, as described in earlier chapters, the client personnel will have a "feel" for the types of solutions that are possible. Having already been informed of the type of facts collected during the fact collection phase and the more interesting aspects of the analysis phase, the client should not be surprised at the scope of the alternative solutions presented for discussion.

During the discussions with the management of the consulting organization and the client it is very helpful to summarize for them the process that was used to synthesize these alternative solutions. This permits the project team to convey an image of being professionally thorough and helps build confidence of management and the client in the alternative solutions presented.

3.12. Select and Describe the Recommended Solution

Sometimes a consultant is fortunate in that the quantitative data collected are definitive enough so that one alternative solution can clearly be documented to provide higher performance at roughly equal cost or equal performance at lower cost. In the event that none of the alternative solutions identified provides a clear-cut advantage over the other alternatives, the consultant may be forced to evaluate the alternative solutions further to be able to recommend any solution.

Some of the techniques that can be used at this time include the following:

- Review the rankings of the quantifiable and nonquantifiable performance characteristics against the evaluation criteria developed.
- Screen the alternative solutions again based on personal judgment.
- Perform a forced choice comparison by weighing the alternatives two at a time.
- Ask key project team members to project the expected results of each alternative and then compare these projections of expected performance.
- And if all of these fail, let the client choose. In some cases a client may specifically not want a recommendation from the consulting organization. In this case the consultant may only present the alternatives and carefully discuss the advantages and disadvantages of each alternative. If the client is going to choose the alternative, the consulting organization should carefully weigh the ethics of allowing this choice to be incorporated in the consultant's report in such a way that it appears to be the consultant's recommendation.

The selected alternative will then be described in terms of:

- The action required.
- The operation of the recommended approach.
- The configuration of the approach.

The description of the selected solution is not the recommendation. Development of the recommendation is described in Chapter 8.

4. CASE STUDY

When Bill decided that the analysis was essentially complete, he called for a review meeting with the project team. At this meeting they review the conclusions developed to date and review the types of solutions that will be needed based on the initial work plan and the conclusions just developed.

The team then discusses the basic relationships that are involved in providing security in a transit organization that includes several jurisdictions. They next discuss the likely motivation of the key groups involved in funding and managing the transit system and its security operation. These key groups include:

- Transit management.
- Transit board.
- Local officials.
- The general public.
- The security organization personnel.

Bill then schedules a meeting from 8:30 A.M. until 9:00 A.M. the next day to brainstorm the subject and attempt to get as many ideas as possible on the table.

The brainstorming session produces numerous ideas related to the transit security program. Bill has these ideas transcribed and distributed to the project team members. He then decides that it will be appropriate for each of the team members to establish a forced choice connector matrix to try to combine several ideas into acceptable alternatives.

Subsequent to these exercises, the project team meets and reduces the possible alternatives to five. Each of the five alternatives is compared to the criteria identified in the problem definition phase and a consensus is developed among the project team as to the most desirable solution.

Bill then discusses these alternatives and the recommended solution in detail with the vice president. He also reviews the working papers and related backup material with the vice president. Subsequent to this review, Bill sits down with the principal client and describes how the five alternatives were developed and thoroughly discusses each alternative with the client. He then indicates to the client the nature of the recommendation that will be forthcoming and the reasons for that recommendation. At this time, Bill and the client have a thorough discussion about the various impacts that these recommendations might have in the client organization and they begin to develop a strategy for how they will present the recommendations and what topics will be emphasized to each client group.

5. SUMMARY

Alternative solutions are obtained by synthesis.

Synthesis is the combining of the constituent elements of the problem into a workable solution.

The type of recommendation needed should shape the development of alternatives.

The basic relationships among the variables and the motivation of the key personnel can provide some useful insights into the shape of the alternatives.

Synthesis techniques include:

- Brainstorming.
- Asking questions.
- Searching the literature.
- Developing an analogy chain.
- Synectics.

The description of each alternative solution will include:

- The action that will be required to implement the solution.
- The operation of that solution.
- The configuration of the solution.

Coordinate the candidate alternatives with your client.

The description of an alternative solution is not a recommendation. The development of recommendations is described in Chapter 8.

CHAPTER EIGHT

Presenting Recommendations

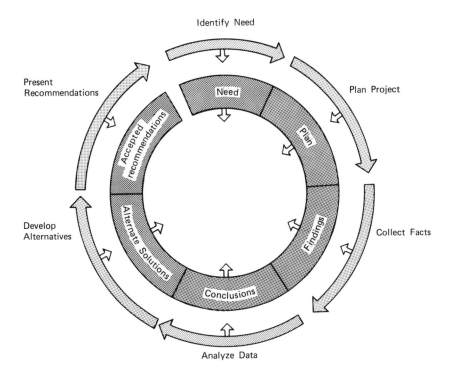

M ost of us have observed projects where technically supportable solutions were never implemented as a result of the methods used by the project team to present their recommendations. This chapter discusses a method of presenting results to clients that will enhance the probability that the recommendations will be accepted and acted on.

Recommendations are prescriptions for action. They may contain innovative ideas but neither the client nor the consultant should expect the recommendations to be some magical breakthrough. Several years ago I was in a client's office when one of his subordinates came rushing in to display the results of one of their contractor's projects. The output was a letter report that described the problem, listed some alternatives, discussed some major considerations, and made a recommendation. The subordinate threw the letter on the boss's desk and said, "I could have told you that." The boss scanned the letter and looked icily at the subordinate and said, "But you didn't." Although the recommendation appeared to be a reasonable solution to the situation, the subordinate seemed to believe that if the recommendation was not a flash of new thought he had never considered, then he had not obtained his money's worth from the consultant. The approaches discussed in this chapter may help reduce this feeling among your less experienced clients.

1. PURPOSE

The purpose of presenting results to your clients is to:

- Communicate the results of the project to your clients so that they will:
  - Understand the findings.
  - Agree with your conclusions.
  - Implement your recommendations.
- Provide tangible documentation for:
  - Implementing the recommendations.
  - Use as a reference document during project implementation.
  - Use by the project team as a reference for future projects and as a permanent record of the consultant's professional development.

The most important measure of the project results is whether the client acted on your recommendation and improved the situation that led to the project in the beginning. As was stated earlier, in all but the most unusual cases, if the client fails to act on your recommendation, you have failed in the project. You have wasted your time and the client's money.

2. PROCESS OF PRESENTING RESULTS

Each project will have to be reviewed carefully at the time the alternative solutions are developed so that a presentation strategy specifically applicable to that project and those clients can be established. The following discussion describes a general process whereby the consultant could present and get acceptance of study results. These steps should be considered by each project team to determine which steps to emphasize and how their situation would be best satisfied.

The following four basic presentation media are available to the consultant to present the project results:

- Counseling.
- Briefings.
- Final reports.
- Meetings.

There are many variations that can be used for each of these four media. The steps that could be taken to present the recommended solution(s) are depicted in Exhibit 8.1. Each of these steps is described in the following paragraphs.

2.1. Review the Recommended Solution

The selected alternative you are recommending should be reviewed carefully to determine the completeness of the alternative and the implications involved. The selected alternative would have already been discussed with your principal clients during the previous phase and at least tentative agreement would have been achieved with your principal clients. This step includes the interpretation of the following steps to fit the actual requirement to present the project results to this client.

2.2. Determine Client Alignments

It is important at this step to determine, or predict, who in the client's organization may be for, against, or neutral with respect to the solution to be im-

EXHIBIT 8.1 Presenting Recommendations

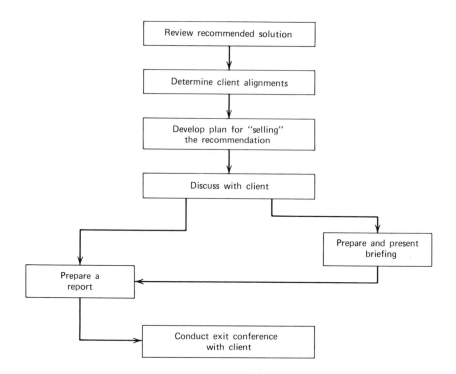

plemented. After identification of each of the client groups and their propensity to accept the solution, one can ask, "Why will the group be disposed toward reacting in that fashion?" and then build on your answers in the development of your selling strategy. For instance, if your immediate client is the Assistant Secretary, or the Office of the Assistant Secretary, and you are working on a problem that relates to or includes a change in data processing functions, a solution that may be quite acceptable to the Assistant Secretary may not be favorably received by the manager of the data processing organization. The data processing manager may not be supportive of a technically good solution for reasons that are not well aligned with the organization's mission. The data processing manager could resist outside comments, be unwilling to accept change of any type, or be reluctant to accept a reduction in size or importance of the data processing organization. The better you can understand these possible reactions, the better your selling strategy can be assembled.

The status quo is usually an alternative in any organization and there is considerable pressure in most organizations to resist change. An organization, or system, when disturbed by an external action, or threat, will move to counteract the change. This basic urge for an organization to resist change should be carefully considered when developing a strategy to present your recommendations.

2.3. Develop a Plan for "Selling" the Recommendation

The concept of developing a "selling" plan for your recommendation is based on two assumptions:

- The recommendation that you have developed is a technically, financially, and socially acceptable solution to the client's need.
- The principal client or clients understand the recommendation and have fully approved the essence of the change to be made.

A carefully thought-out plan for structuring the recommendations and the method of communication of these recommendations to the various client groups can have a significant impact on the implementation. The factors that should be thought out and included in the plan are:

- The structure and timing of the action items in the recommendation itself. After assessing the likely responses of the groups involved, it may be necessary to make adjustments to the solution to be recommended, which will not be significant in terms of the technical impact of the recommendation but may be significant in how they are perceived and accepted by a particular group. The timing of the implementation steps may also be able to be adjusted to make the solution more acceptable to some group if the change in schedule has a low impact on the overall recommended program.
- Determine the type and timing of the presentation media to be used. Develop a formal or informal plan indicating the content, the participants, and the format of the methods to be used to communicate the recommendation to the client. A useful element in discussing the recommendation with neutral clients, or clients you expect to be somewhat unfavorable to the implementation of the recommendation, is to include those clients in carefully planned counselling sessions before the structure of the recommendation is cast in concrete. These sessions could be performed by using one or two members of the project team who have the best relationship with that individual to sit down and discuss the situation, the objectives of the solution, and the positive and negative impacts on the individual and

their organization. Proper use of the counselling technique early enough in the process of developing the recommendation can modify the perception on the part of client groups and change their willingness to accept the recommended solution.

The use of briefings or general meetings before preparation and promulgation of the report containing the recommendation can also be a useful tool.

2.4. Discuss the Selling Plan with the Client

It is important that your principal client thoroughly understand and agree with your plan for selling the recommendations in the organization. It should not be necessary to sell the principal client at this time since that individual or individuals should have been deeply involved in each phase of the consulting process and have "bought" the recommended solution earlier in the project.

2.5. Develop and Present a Project Briefing

The purpose of the project briefing is to present the complete recommendation and supporting material to a larger group of clients at one time to be able to confirm the earlier private discussions and to obtain group consensus on the action to be taken. The objective of the briefing is to communicate to the audience what is recommended, why it is important, and what the benefits to them are in taking this action. This briefing can also be used to iron out any planned or unknown questions that might remain. It is important to select the correct group of participants to be in this audience. The audience should include all of the major and other clients that will be involved in the approval, funding, or operation of the action being recommended. The dynamics of your client's situation will determine whether several briefings will be needed, or will be more effective than a single large briefing.

Once the audience for a particular briefing has been established, it is useful to consider the background and interest of the people attending; you can thus shape the presentation to fit that collection of backgrounds and interests. Sufficient planning is necessary at this point to try to have the presentation style and format shaped as best it can be to reinforce the understanding already reached with the participants during the private discussions. Insufficient planning of this final presentation may have hidden costs that are far in excess of the direct time and material cost of developing a good presentation. These costs could include the projection of a confused or disorganized image, which could lead to suspicion regarding the validity of the recommendation and result in a reduction of commitment on the part of some officials in the client organization. This reduction could result in the recommendations not being accepted.

The types of considerations that need to be addressed are:

- The physical environment available for the presentation. This would include the size, shape, and location of the presentation room needed or the one that is available.
- The psychological mood of the audience. The number of friendly, unfriendly, or skeptical persons in the audience can have a significant impact on the way the briefing is structured.
- The length of the presentation. How much time do you need during the briefing to present the material to make the case that you would like to make? How much time can this audience devote to this subject?
- Relationship to other presentations. Are there other briefings or meetings on the schedule of this audience that may influence the frame of mind of the participants?
- Time of day. What time during the day would be the most appropriate time to present this subject to this audience? What time during the day has been scheduled for this presentation? Can this time be modified if it is desired?

The style of the briefing will have to be structured to match the needs of this audience on this subject. However, there are some general guidelines for any presentation. Structure your presentation and your style based on the assumption that the audience is intelligent but uninformed. Structuring a presentation with this in mind should discourage a tendency to talk "down" to or "over the head" of the audience.

Visual aids have been recognized for some time as being a very effective support to almost any attempt at communication between people. The kinds of visual aids selected will be based on many factors, including the characteristics of the audience discussed above, the size and the shape and the seating arrangement of the room, and the length of time available for the presentation. A broad range of visual aids are available to the person or persons delivering the briefing. These include:

- Flip charts.
- Chalkboards.

- Hard poster boards.
- Static projection techniques using such methods as:
  - Viewgraphs.
  - Slides.
  - Filmstrips.
- Dynamic presentation such as movies and videotapes.
- Three-dimensional displays such as examples, mock-ups, models, and simulations.
- Combinations of these techniques.

A large body of information has been published regarding the techniques of presentation. (Refer to the bibliography for a sampling of books containing detailed discussions of oral presentations.)

2.6. Prepare a Final Report

You have now performed a study in response to your client's needs, developed alternative recommendations, selected (in conjunction with your client) a solution to be implemented, and carefully coordinated this recommended solution with your client. You are now ready to begin preparation of your final report. (There are situations for which the preparation of a final report may not be the correct approach, but even in those cases, the action being recommended would be thoroughly documented.

The report outline was developed during the project planning stage at the beginning of the project and has likely been refined during the course of the project. Even after that detailed planning and attention to the report content during the course of the project, it is still appropriate to pause at this point and take the time to again review the nature of the message that you wish to convey.

The preparation for and production of the final report is described in the following paragraphs on:

- Planning the report.
- Drafting a writing outline.
- Reviewing the writing outline.
- Writing the final report.

PLANNING THE REPORT

The report planning can be enhanced by consideration of several questions. These questions include:

- Who will approve this final report (i.e., the action recommended)?
- On what basis will the approving official approve the recommendations in this report?
- Who will use the system to be implemented as a result of the recommendations?
- What will the users expect to see in this report?
- Who must concur with the recommendations for action included in this report and what will those concurring officials expect to see in the report?
- What should not be in the report? Is there some point or characteristic of the organization or the system being recommended that should be left out of the description? It is possible to encounter a situation in which including some information in the report contributes little but may have significant negative impact.
- Who needs an executive summary? Is the opinion, or action, of those people who need an executive summary germane enough to the implementation of the recommendation that it justifies the development of an executive summary?
- What would the client like to hear in this report?
- What points do the project team feel must be made in the report?

After consideration of these types of questions, the organization, format, and style of the report should be confirmed and the basic outline that was generated during the planning phase should be modified as appropriate.

The final step during the report planning period is to assemble the findings worksheets, relevant data, the analysis worksheets, synthesis worksheets, and the description of the recommended alternative solution by chapter and subchapter of the outline of the final report.

DRAFTING A WRITING OUTLINE FOR THE FINAL REPORT

You now have your chapter outline, the subchapter headings, and the format and style of the report established. In most cases the report will now consist of:

- An introductory chapter.

- Three to five chapters providing appropriate detail on the subject under study.
- A chapter presenting the recommendations for action.

The development of the writing outline would carry your report to the next level of depth. Usually the development of the writing outline would be assigned to the appropriate project staff persons responsible for a particular technical area or for that chapter of the report. One effective way to get the writing outline produced is to request the assigned staff person to develop a tentative writing outline for his or her chapter. This chapter writing outline would be no more than two or three pages and would indicate the major subjects in each chapter in a logical sequence. This might include:

- Introductory statement.
- A concluding statement for that chapter or subject.
- Three to four additional topics that will be presented in the body of the chapter.

There are several considerations that may be helpful in focusing on the most appropriate structure for that chapter. These considerations include:

- What is the audience for this chapter?
- What is the objective for this chapter?
- What action do you expect the reader to take based on this chapter?
- How can this chapter affect the action to be taken or its timing?
- What is the central theme of this chapter?
- If your client asked you to tell him or her, in one minute, what is in this chapter, what would you say?
- How does the central theme of this chapter relate to the general theme of the final report?
- What are the major elements of the central theme of this chapter?
- What subsections to the chapter are necessary to respond to each of the major elements of the chapter theme?
- What important points do you want the reader to understand, concur with, and take action on regarding each element listed?

When these questions are resolved, the consultant should have a two- to three-page outline of the chapter filled with dots, dashes, and so on, that will convey the essence of that chapter. This chapter writing outline is now ready for review.

REVIEWING THE WRITING OUTLINE

When the writing outlines for each chapter have been drafted, the first level of review is among the project team members, in concert with the project manager, to ensure that the report has an acceptable level of consistency from beginning to end. This consistency has been described as "flowing and growing." In other words, does the report begin by clearly stating the need(s) addressed? Does each chapter pick up this theme and continue in a logical expansion of the theme? Does the presentation of alternative solutions clearly flow out of the earlier chapters?

The second level of review, for a consulting firm, will be with the internal management of the consulting organization. This review would include the corporate officials, or the partners, in charge of this project. This review normally would be done with the project manager presenting the material, with the support of the project team members, to the management officials for their review and approval. The documents that normally would be forthcoming and the order in which they might be presented are as follows:

- The contract document.
- The original statement of client need.
- The original report outline with key questions.
- The findings worksheets.
- The analysis worksheets.
- The synthesis worksheets.
- The recommended action.
- The final chapter writing outlines.

After a discussion of the chapter writing outlines, and after it has been established that the chapter writing outlines appropriately respond to the contract and the statement of need and are based on the solid documentation listed above, the management officials would approve or approve with changes, and sign off on the writing outlines.

The third level of review of the chapter writing outlines will be to formally or informally present these to your client for their review and comment. In most cases this review would be an informal discussion of the chapter writing outline with the key clients to ensure that all the relevant points will be covered in the report. The amount of the documentation listed above that would be presented and reviewed by the client is a matter left to the judgment of the project manager and the management officials.

WRITING THE FINAL REPORT

After the acceptance of the recommendation and the approval of the detailed chapter writing outlines, you are now ready to write your final report. This section presents some general comments regarding recommendations and writing style. The techniques of good writing are described in numerous texts and other publications (see the bibliography for this chapter).

Recommendations. A recommendation is your prescription for action. It is the action that you have developed to solve the problem that the client retained you for in the first place. It is the central focus of the entire report. Recommendations should always include answers to the following questions:

- What is prescribed? Tell the reader exactly what action you are recommending be taken to solve the client's needs. Provide a clear description of the topic and central theme of the solution recommended.
- Why is this action important? Most recommended actions will require resources, redirections, and energy on the part of those people who will take the action. They must be convinced that the issues involved are important enough to justify the discomfort associated with this, or any, action.
- What are the benefits? Rarely will people do anything simply because you tell them, or even suggest they do so. Even though you may be a high or modestly priced consultant, it is totally unreasonable to expect that people will do anything simply because you tell them to do so. There must be some benefit to most, if not all, the people involved. If you cannot identify and describe the benefits of taking this action, you may have missed the mark and maybe the recommended action should not be taken after all.

Recommendations may include, depending on the judgment of the project manager and the client, answers to the following questions:

- Who should take this action? The official or organization that will have the responsibility to implement the prescribed action may be identified in the recommendation.

- How can the prescribed action be accomplished? You may describe the tasks necessary to implement the described action.
- What resources are required? It may be appropriate to include an estimate of the resources needed to implement the described action.

The foregoing questions may be used to provide a checklist for evaluating draft recommendations.

Writing Style. Writing style is a complex subject that has been discussed extensively in the literature. A very important point to keep in mind when writing your final report is to focus on an intelligent but uninformed audience. This concept may prevent you from entering into an absurd level of detail and explanation at one end of the spectrum and carelessly using acronyms and slang at the other end of the spectrum. The second guideline suggested is that you make every attempt to write as clearly as you can. If you have thoroughly covered the subject under study and sincerely believe what you are writing, then try to write clearly and understandably. Visualize how you would explain it to a friend over a cup of coffee.

2.7. Conduct an Exit Conference

After your report has been prepared, and in some cases delivered to the client in draft form for his review and comments, and the final report and any other documentation or products have been delivered, it is appropriate to conduct an exit conference. An exit conference provides the opportunity to:

- Allow the client to ask any remaining questions in a fairly formal setting.
- Review once more with the client the actions that must be taken to implement the recommendation.
- Convey to the client that this is the end of your work: you have concluded the work that you have set out to do and are turning over to him or her the responsibility for all future action on this project.

The exit conference is also an appropriate forum to discuss possibilities for additional consulting work to respond to any other important needs that should be addressed and may have been identified during the course of the project.

3. CASE STUDY

After the details of the major recommendations are outlined, but before the report is written, Bill again sits down and has a long discussion with the principal client so they can carefully go over the principal findings, the major conclusions, and the implications of the recommendations. Each recommendation is discussed in detail to explain to the client exactly what is being recommended and what Bill knows of the impacts of this recommendation on the client organization.

Bill next discusses with the client his recommended method of presenting these recommendations to the client organization and other interested groups.

He then reviews with the client the detailed writing outline that has been prepared to describe the final report. The vice president participates in all of these discussions.

It is decided that it will be appropriate to hold a series of briefings for the client organization as well as for the committees representing the three public safety services involved.

After completion of the briefings and resolution of all the questions that came up during those briefings, the project team writes the final report. A typical example of one recommendation is presented in Exhibit 8.2.

The report draft is carefully reviewed by the project manager with each of the key project team members. Each substantive statement of fact made in the

EXHIBIT 8.2 Case Study Notes for Presenting Recommendations

Typical Recommendation

Title—Establish a Security Organization

The transit organization should accept the full responsibility for, and establish a security organization to: patrol transit vehicles, provide revenue protection, and provide surveillance for transit headquarters and yards.

It is important that a transit security organization conduct these operations so that the organization can establish firm control over the central core of operations and push to establish a positive image with the general public.

The benefits of establishing this type of organization will be strong management control over key operations and the fare revenue. In addition, this approach will provide a lower overall security cost by emphasizing transit control over key functions and utilizing local agencies to perform those services for which they are generally staffed and trained to perform.

report is cross-referenced in the left margin to the page of the work papers where the source data for that statement are located. When the project manager finishes his review and recycles the report through the report department, he makes the project work papers available to the vice president for the vice president to review the report.

After completing the internal reviews, the project manager provides a copy of the draft report to the client for review. Bill meets with the client after a few days and carefully discusses with him each of the major points that he has developed during his review. Bill then brings back the marked-up copy from the client and uses that as a basis for the final internal edit of the report. The marked-up copy returned from the client is labeled in ink and very carefully filed away in the project files. This marked-up copy provides clear and legally binding evidence that the client reviewed the work and had no objections to the work other than those that he made in the markup, which were resolved.

A short time after delivery of all of the contractually required copies of the project report, Bill and the vice president schedule a meeting with the client for the exit conference. At this conference the work to be done is reiterated, the results achieved are repeated, the actions to be taken by the client organization are reviewed, and the point is carefully but firmly emphasized that the firm has completed its work and all subsequent action on this topic will be the responsibility of the client organization.

The vice president suggested that if the client encountered difficulty with the two most troublesome portions of the implementation program, his firm will be quite pleased to return and talk with the client about the services that could be provided under a new project.

4. SUMMARY

A recommendation is a prescription for action on the part of your client. The decision(s) that you recommend to your client will be to get something to happen that may not have happened or to prevent something from happening that would probably have taken place.

The purpose of communicating the results of the project to the client is so that the client will:

• Understand the findings.
• Agree with the conclusions.
• Implement the recommendations.

The most commonly used media for presenting results are:

- Counseling.
- Briefings.
- Final reports.
- Meetings.

Recommendations should always include:

- What is prescribed.
- Why this action is important.
- What the benefits are.

The recommendations may include:

- Who should take the action.
- How it can be implemented.
- What resources are required.

The goal of all the media used to communicate the results should be to communicate with an intelligent but uninformed audience.

CHAPTER NINE

Providing Implementation Assistance

O ften the consultant who performs a study and develops the recommendation for action is requested to participate in the implementation of that action. This chapter provides some general guidance on deciding if and how the consultant should participate in the implementation phase.

1. PURPOSE OF IMPLEMENTATION ASSISTANCE

The purpose of providing implementation assistance to a client is to assist the client in implementing the recommended action(s) that will satisfy the basic need. The assistance provided may complement the client's staff or the consultant may have the overall responsibility for implementation.

2. WHEN TO RECOMMEND ASSISTANCE

The decision on the part of the consulting organization to recommend implementation assistance is sometimes a very difficult one and often places the integrity of the consulting organization in clear focus. The countervailing pressures are: (1) to recommend that the client expend resources for outside assistance only to do things that can best be done by an outside organization, and (2), on the other hand, to acquire additional business is a basic interest in consulting organizations.

There are times when it makes good sense for the consultant to continue into the implementation period to assist the client in implementing the solution. These situations include:

- When new technology is being introduced into the organization and it is unreasonable to expect the internal staff to assimilate and effectively use this new technology during the initial period of implementation.
- When insufficient client staff is available to be able to provide the basic manpower required to implement the solution.
- When there are key client staff skills that are missing as a result of client personnel turnover, client training programs, or other reasons.
- When the solution includes a hard schedule deadline that must be met, and the impact on the organization if the deadline is not met is significant.
- When the pressure for a high level of performance from the solution on the first attempt makes retaining outside consultants a worthwhile insurance policy.

148

Another general guideline is that for a consulting organization to recommend to its client that they provide some form of implementation assistance, the consulting organizations should be in the position to be able to do that task better than, or as well as, anyone else who may be available to the client to do that task. If it doesn't make sense for either party, it should not be done.

The following story illustrates the difficulties that can develop in defining implementation programs. A large national consulting firm brought in a staff person from an East Coast operation to do a three-day task on a large project for one of its western clients. On the afternoon of the second day that person and the project leader in the western office were discussing alternatives for implementing that part of the study. The manager in charge of the office entered the room and listened to the discussion for a few minutes and then stated, "Well, that's all very good but what have we built in for follow-on for ourselves?" After a little hemming and hawing the discussion continued without answering the question of the manager. A very short time later the manager interrupted again with the same question. At that time, the consultant from the eastern office stated that it was his policy to carefully assess the needs of the client and then determine what the client needed to be able to solve the problems that were being studied. After the action items that needed to be done were identified, then those items could be reviewed to determine which, if any, of those items could be performed by the consulting firm better than, or as well as, anyone else. Then he would be in a position to make a recommendation to the client about participating in the implementation. After a short pause the manager said, "Certainly, that is correct," and the conversation continued for about one more minute and the manager interrupted again by saying, "Well, this is all very interesting but what have we built in for follow-on for ourselves?" The manager appeared to be placing his interest in acquiring business above the interests of his client.

3. TYPES OF IMPLEMENTATION ASSISTANCE

There is a broad range of levels of involvement that the consulting organization can participate in during the implementation period. These levels of implementation assistance include:

- *Turnkey systems.* For a turnkey system, the consultant would accept the complete responsibility for detail design, implementation, operation, training, and turnover of a working system to the client. It would be the consultant's responsibility to identify and solve all the interface problems, install the necessary equipment, debug the operation, and figuratively hand the client the key to a working system.

- *Some client involvement.* In this case the consulting organization would accept the majority of the responsibility for the implementation program but some tasks would be performed by client personnel. It is most important that this type of implementation be very carefully defined so that the interface between what the client is supposed to do and what the consulting organization is supposed to do does not become an issue at a later time when schedule adherence or level of performance is in question.

- *Technical advisors.* In this role, the consulting organization would provide technical advisors to assist the client personnel on a regular basis but the actual work would be performed by client personnel and the client would be responsible for the implementation program.

- *Technical reviews.* In this case, the consulting organization would participate in periodic technical reviews where the progress, problems, and planned activity of the implementation program would be discussed.

- *On-call assistance.* This is obviously a low level of consulting participation in the implementation program. It simply consists of being willing to respond to client questions in the event that difficulties arise during the implementation period. It may consist of telephone consultations, answering correspondence, or actually visiting the client to provide direction and information.

4. SUMMARY

The client and the consultant should be aware that the consultant is under the countervailing pressures of (1) wanting to recommend only that additional work which needs to be done outside and (2) wanting to acquire additional consulting business.

The types of consultant assistance in project implementation include:

- Turnkey systems.
- Some client involvement.
- Technical advisors.
- Technical reviews.
- On-call assistance.

CHAPTER TEN
Evaluating the Results

One principal form of professional growth is learning from past activity. In the consulting or engineering field, an important part of learning is the examination of completed projects to determine what went well, what did not go so well, and what would be done differently if another opportunity presented itself to perform that type of project again.

A way to obtain the feedback that is useful for learning from prior consulting projects is to conduct an evaluation of the project.

The process commonly called evaluation is a method of examining a project to determine the effectiveness with which the implemented solution(s) satisfied the project objectives. The evaluation is usually carried out in accordance with a structured evaluation plan with the goal of identifying potential project improvements.

A formal evaluation of a large project, or program, may be quite a large project itself. The evaluation that a consulting organization might make of a completed project would be similar in structure but obviously would be scaled down substantially. A consulting organization would be performing the project evaluation on an unpaid, self-initiated basis primarily for professional development purposes. However, a project team that initially designed a system will usually be able to quickly assess the progress toward achieving the major objectives of that project.

1. PURPOSE OF EVALUATION

The purpose of evaluation has been broken into the following three categories:

- To review the results of the project activity and the recommendations made to obtain a better understanding of how the client was able to implement the recommendations and how those recommendations actually worked. Topics for follow-up counseling with the client may be identified.
- To obtain feedback on the conduct of the work and the quality of the recommendations so that the training program for the internal consulting staff may be adjusted.
- To identify new problems that should be addressed for the client. Project evaluations often identify topics that can be brought to the attention of the management of the client organization and might be the basis of a new consulting project. This, of course, would allow the consultant to start the consulting process all over again with a newly defined situation.

2. WHEN TO EVALUATE

It would seem that project evaluations are probably best considered in a two-stage program. The first stage would be two to four weeks after the project is formally over and the reports delivered. At this time, the evaluation would cover those activities performed on the projects, the client situation encountered, and other matters that could be discussed at that point. The second phase of the evaluation would be a much less formal evaluation, which could take place only after enough time had passed to allow the recommendations to be implemented and some feedback information to be available in the client organization. This feedback would be obtained from the operation of the recommended system so that its effectiveness could be assessed.

3. WHAT TO EVALUATE

There are many structures one could use to shape an evaluation of a completed project. The structure that seems to be the most relevant is to divide the considerations into the following factors:

- Client satisfaction.
- Technical performance.
- Staff performance.

Each of these is briefly discussed below.

3.1. Client Satisfaction

One way for a consulting organization to evaluate the effectiveness of prior recommendations and system designs is to assess the level of client satisfaction. At the end of the project implementation, the client's impression may be based on its expectations of what the system is projected to do. A later evaluation will permit the client to obtain a substantial amount of operating results and determine how well the recommendations are working.

The client's satisfaction could be determined by asking questions such as:

- Were the recommendations implemented?
- To what extent were the recommendations implemented?

- What did the client(s) tell you about their level of satisfaction?
- What did the client(s) tell others about the project?
- What did the client say about his or her willingness to work with your organization again?
- Has the client awarded to you or discussed with your organization any additional pending work?

These questions would be used to frame further questions for your client, for the project team, and for outside parties familiar with the client organization.

3.2. Technical Performance

This factor concentrates on how well the actual system, process, or procedure recommended has satisfied the design objectives. The technical performance investigation may include the following questions:

- If the recommendations were implemented, did they work?
- How well did they work?
- What revision had to be made after the initial implementation?
- How well did the recommended solution satisfy the stated need?
- Were the project results technically complete, accurate, and within the scope of the project?
- Was client and management concurrence obtained and documented at appropriate points in the project?
- Were the results presented so that the client and others could readily use those results?
- Was the schedule met?
- If the schedule was not met, why not?
- Was the resource allocation plan for the project adhered to?
- If the resource allocation plan was not adhered to, why not?
- What were the most successful management, data collection, and analysis techniques?
- What were the least successful management, data collection, and analysis techniques?
- What would be done differently for a similar project?

3.3 Staff Performance

This factor is intended to obtain information about the performance of the project and client personnel during the course of the project. Some of the questions that could be used to obtain this information are:

- What needed skills were not available at the quality required by the project?
- Were these skills of the type that project team members should have possessed?
- Were these skill level discrepancies discussed with appropriate project team members?
- Has a plan been developed to improve these skills within the organization?
- What skills were well executed by the project team?
- Were these outstanding skills discussed with appropriate project personnel?
- Was the good performance recorded in the person's personnel file?
- Were any skill deficiencies identified in the client organization?
- Were these skill deficiencies communicated to client management?
- Were the well-executed skills and the not-so-well-executed skills communicated to the firm's training director?

4. PROCESS OF EVALUATION

The process used to evaluate projects varies widely depending on the nature and complexity of the project. A general sequence of steps that can be used to evaluate projects resembles many steps in the overall consulting process. The steps, which are depicted in Exhibit 10.1, include:

- *Review the objectives of the project at the beginning.* This would include a review of the statement of need and the basic issues, constraints, assumptions, and objectives as identified in the statement of need. The client's request for proposal and other initial client documentation should be reviewed.
- *Develop a plan for the evaluation.* On a very large project this plan might be a few-page memo. For a small or medium-sized project it simply may be some mental notes that one would review that project's basic scope,

EXHIBIT 10.1   Evaluation of the Results

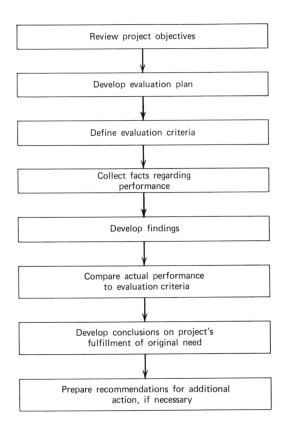

```
┌─────────────────────────────────────────┐
│         Review project objectives        │
└─────────────────────────────────────────┘
                     │
                     ▼
┌─────────────────────────────────────────┐
│          Develop evaluation plan          │
└─────────────────────────────────────────┘
                     │
                     ▼
┌─────────────────────────────────────────┐
│          Define evaluation criteria       │
└─────────────────────────────────────────┘
                     │
                     ▼
┌─────────────────────────────────────────┐
│         Collect facts regarding           │
│                performance                │
└─────────────────────────────────────────┘
                     │
                     ▼
┌─────────────────────────────────────────┐
│              Develop findings             │
└─────────────────────────────────────────┘
                     │
                     ▼
┌─────────────────────────────────────────┐
│        Compare actual performance         │
│           to evaluation criteria          │
└─────────────────────────────────────────┘
                     │
                     ▼
┌─────────────────────────────────────────┐
│      Develop conclusions on project's     │
│        fulfillment of original need       │
└─────────────────────────────────────────┘
                     │
                     ▼
┌─────────────────────────────────────────┐
│   Prepare recommendations for additional  │
│            action, if necessary           │
└─────────────────────────────────────────┘
```

look at the final report, and visit with the client to determine how the recommendations turned out.

- *Define evaluation criteria that are relevant for that project.* If it is an evaluation of the success of your recommendations, then a measure of how the implemented system is now working must be established. Measures could include such parameters as employee turnover, customer complaints, profits, costs, and error rates, depending on the nature of the project.

- *Collect the facts necessary for the evaluation.* In some cases, this information may be gained by telephone discussions or personal visits to the client to discuss how the system works, what difficulties have been identified, or what changes the client would make given the opportunity to do the project over again. In other cases, fact collection may require going back and collecting error rates, the amount of outage time, through-put rates, costs, and so on.

- *Develop findings from these facts.* This step would consist of consolidating the data collected and turning these data into meaningful statements of fact.

- *Compare the actual performance with the evaluation criteria selected.* The formality of this step would obviously vary substantially depending on the size or complexity of the project. However, it is a step that should always be included in project evaluation.

- *Develop conclusions regarding the level of satisfaction of the objectives of the project.* This is the step in the evaluation process where the judgment of the consultant is heavily involved. At this point you can phrase statements that describe the degree of satisfaction of the initial project objectives and, probably, the causes for any lack of performance.

- *Develop recommendations for action.* Usually there are some action items that result from a project evaluation. In the best case, it would be the positive feedback to communicate to the client, to the project staff that did the job, and to management in the consulting organization that the project was reviewed and the recommendations were working satisfactorily.

Any situation identified during this project evaluation which had a significant negative impact on the performance of the system should be discussed with the client. These discussions with the client will determine if further consulting assistance is required to develop mechanisms to allow the system to achieve original performance objectives.

In most evaluations, there would be some feedback available for input into the requirements for subsequent training for the consulting staff.

The project manager, or other person responsible for the evaluation, may document the findings, conclusions, and recommendations in a small report or in a memorandum. The report should be distributed to the project team, the manager(s) of the consulting organization, the firm's training director, and possibly to the client.

5. SUMMARY

It is necessary for consulting organizations to obtain regular feedback on how well their recommendations are working for their clients. The feedback may be obtained by conducting one evaluation immediately after completion of the project and a second evaluation after the recommended actions have been taken.

The evaluation will help identify difficulties encountered with the recommendations, new problems in the client organization, and training needs for the consulting staff. The end product of the evaluation is a small report or memorandum describing the actions to be taken.

CHAPTER ELEVEN

Summary

T he purpose of this book was to describe a generalized process of problem solving in formal consulting projects. In addition, a step-by-step example project was to be provided as a case study accompanying each major chapter.

In the preceding chapters, the following ideas were discussed:

- Identifying the need leads to a statement of need.
- Planning the project leads to a project work plan.
- Collecting the facts leads to findings.
- Analyzing the findings leads to conclusions.
- Synthesizing leads to alternative solutions.
- Comparing alternative solutions leads to recommendations.

Another way to look at the structure of the consulting process is to start with the end product, the recommendations, and indicate what each step is based on. This structure is depicted in Exhibit 11.1. The structure indicates that:

- Recommendations are the best, or the most acceptable, of the available alternative solutions.
- Synthesis techniques are used to generate the alternative solutions.
- The types of alternative solution developed are shaped by the conclusions.
- Conclusions flow from the judgment of the consultant about the meaning of the findings.
- Findings are drawn from the facts.

In the introduction, it was stated that the benefits of this consulting process were:

- Better quality results from projects, which result from:
  - Forced initial focus on the issues, constraints, and the like.
  - Thorough initial plans for the outputs to be developed.
  - An auditable linkage from source data, to findings, to conclusions, to alternatives, to recommendations.
  - Coordinated recommendations based on documented workpapers.
- Better control of the work done for the individual engineer, the project manager, the company management, and the client, all resulting from:
  - The initial definition of the issues and assumptions and the presentation of these to management and the client for approval.

**EXHIBIT 11.1   The Structure of
the Consulting Process**

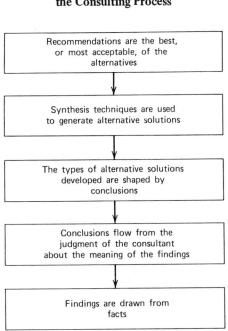

- The definition of specific interim steps (work plan, findings, etc.) that will be presented to management and the client for approval.
- Reduced time demands on the part of the project staff and project management. These reduced time demands, for equivalent quality, result from:
  - The development of up-front agreements defining what each participant will produce.
  - More efficient communications as a result of the clearer definition of project activity.
  - Better defined expectations regarding what will be developed.
  - Fewer last-minute crises.

In the introduction, the following four elements of problem solving were discussed:

- A process for doing the work.
- Technical skills required for the subject under study.

- Human relations skills.
- Drive and motivation.

It is each individual's personal responsibility to define his or her professional goals and determine the degree of expertise that is required in each of these four areas to achieve those goals. Your organization can provide some assistance in terms of liberal training programs, tuition reimbursement, or some time off from the job to follow up on your professional development program. However, it is not the organization's responsibility to see that you achieve your professional goals. If the organization assists, good, but if you are to achieve high professional stature, it is your responsibility to define and implement your personal training program.

There are a number of excellent references on defining one's goals and providing tips for achieving those goals. Several of these are included in the bibliography. Some brief suggestions are presented here for each of the four elements of our approach to problem solving.

A Problem Solving Process. This book can provide a starting point for your development of a process that fits the field in which you want to work. Other types of processes have been defined which may be more relevant to your organization or situation. In any event, it is advisable for you to study this, or any other process, and determine exactly what needs to be modified to fit your situation.

Technical Skills. The development and maintenance of technical skills for your professional growth can be enhanced by several simple steps. The first is to define your personal interests and the interests of your organization to determine what fields you would like to participate in and how those fields coincide with the organization's goals. You can then develop a plan for the topics in which you would like to concentrate your work and self-training program. These topics of concentration will allow you to define specific skills required in the medium and the short run. After you have defined the skills that you would like to possess, and the time in which you think they will be needed, you may then develop a specific self-development program.

Human Relations Skills. Human relations skills is a subject most of us should devote a considerable amount of effort to. No matter how effective we believe we are in our dealings with other people, there is always room for improvement. A constant process of learning and reassessment of your interpersonal relationships is required in a steadily changing environment. This topic too can benefit from a frank assessment of skills that you have. Several published guides can support this type of self-assessment. This can lead you to establishing some goals for improving these skills and to identifying specific formal and/or self-teaching programs to obtain this improvement.

Drive or Motivation. Sometimes it seems that people with drive appear to have been born with the capacity to focus clearly on their objectives. In some cases this may be so, but drive can be improved by a frank assessment of your personal and professional goals. This assessment will allow you to focus your energies much more than if you are wandering through your professional life responding to random job offers and work assignments. Just try the process of establishing some reasonable, achievable goal and giving it a high enough priority in your allocation of time and you may be amazed by the results. A second major element of drive is to develop the ability to conserve your energy. This applies to your interpersonal relationships first. This is the largest waste of personal energy. If you can learn to observe your attitude at those times when you are in a conflict situation, you can just feel your energy slipping away. There are several good references on conserving personal energy in the bibliography.

Please use caution in the application of this approach to your project. Do not attempt to meticulously follow this process, or any other process, but determine exactly what is required for your situation.

For this consulting process or any process to work effectively, it requires the participation of the project staff, the project manager, the consulting organization management, and the client. If any one of those groups does not understand the framework, or refuses to accept responsibility, it will be more difficult to conduct successful projects.

This problem solving process can provide a conceptual approach for conducting technical or management consulting projects. I believe that an understanding of a process like this will permit each consultant, engineer, project manager, or buyer of consulting services to have a mental framework about the logic through which projects should flow. This mental framework can permit the seller and the buyer of consulting services to understand what should be done and to evaluate what has been done. I believe that it is important for each consultant, each engineer, each manager, and each consulting organization to strive to improve the methods by which consulting services are provided.

Bibliography

CHAPTER 1. INTRODUCTION

Ackoff, Russel L. *The Art of Problem Solving.* New York: Wiley, 1978.

CHAPTER 2. A PROBLEM SOLVING PROCESS

De Bono, Edward, *New Think.* New York: Basic Books, 1967.

Robertshaw, Joseph E., Stephen J. Mecca, and Mark N. Rerick. *Problem Solving.* Princeton, N.J.: Petrocelli, 1978.

Weinberg, Gerald M. *An Introduction to General Systems Thinking.* New York: Wiley, 1975.

CHAPTER 3. IDENTIFYING THE NEED

Drucker, Peter F. *Management.* New York: Harper & Row, 1973.

Kaufman, Robert. *Identifying and Solving Problems.* LaJolla, Calif.: University Associates, 1979.

Mager, Robert F. *Analyzing Performance Problems.* Belmont, Calif.: Fearon, 1970.

Mager, Robert F. *Goal Analysis.* Belmont, Calif.: Fearon, 1972.

Magerison, Charles. *Managerial Problem Solving.* New York: McGraw-Hill, 1974.

CHAPTER 4. PLANNING THE PROJECT

Albert, Kenneth J. *How To Be Your Own Management Consultant.* New York: McGraw-Hill, 1978.

Hajek, Victor G. *Management of Engineering Projects.* New York: McGraw-Hill, 1977.

Jackson, Keith F. *The Art of Solving Problems.* New York: St. Martins, 1975.

Kerzner, Harold. *Project Management.* Princeton, N.J.: Van Nostrand-Reinhold, 1979.

Kubr, M. *Management Consulting.* Geneva: International Labour Office, 1976.

165

Lippitt, Gordon, and Ronald Lippitt. *The Consulting Process in Action.* LaJolla, Calif.: University Associates, 1978.

McCay, James T. *The Management of Time,* Englewood Cliffs, N.J.: Prentice-Hall, 1959.

Ross, Joel E. *Managing Productivity.* Reston, Va.: Reston, 1977.

Silverman, Melvin. *Project Management.* New York: Wiley, 1976.

Swann, Gloria Harrington. *Top-Down Structured Programming.* Princeton, N.J.: Petrocelli, 1978.

CHAPTER 5. COLLECTING THE FACTS

Albert, Kenneth J. *Handbook of Business Problem Solving.* New York: McGraw-Hill, 1980.

Backstrom, Charles H., and Gerald D. Hursh. *Survey Research.* Evanston, Ill.: Northwestern University Press, 1963.

Blankenship, Albert B. *Professional Telephone Surveys.* New York, McGraw-Hill, 1977.

Cribbin, James J. *Effective Managerial Leadership.* New York: American Management Association, 1972.

Dillman, Don A. *Mail and Telephone Surveys.* New York: Wiley, 1978.

Maynard, Harold B. *Industrial Engineering Handbook.* New York: McGraw-Hill, 1971.

Metzler, Ken. *Creative Interviewing.* Englewood Cliffs, N.J.: Prentice-Hall, 1977.

Molloy, John T. *Dress for Success.* New York: Wyden, 1975.

Oppenheim, A. N. *Questionnaire Design and Attitude Measurement.* New York: Basic Books, 1966.

Sanderson, Michael. *Successful Problem Management.* New York: Wiley-Interscience, 1979.

CHAPTER 6. ANALYZING THE SITUATION

Anthony, Robert N. *Management Accounting.* Homewood, Ill.: Richard D. Irwin, 1956.

Box, G. E. P., and G. M. Jenkins, *Time Series Analysis, Forecasting and Control.* San Francisco: Holden-Day, 1976.

Buffa, Edward S. *Modern Production Management.* New York: Wiley, 1961.

Cyert, R. M., and H. Justin Davidson. *Statistical Sampling for Accounting Information.* Englewood Cliffs, N.J.: Prentice-Hall, 1962.

LaPatra, Jack W. *Applying the Systems Approach to Urban Development.* Stroudsburg, Pa.: Dowden, Hutchinson & Ross, 1973.

Makridakis, Spyros and W. C. Wheelwright, *Forecasting.* New York: Wiley, 1978.

Martin, James. *Systems Analysis for Data Transmission.* Englewood Cliffs, N.J.: Prentice-Hall, 1972.

Moder, Joseph J., and Salah E. Elmaghraby. *Handbook of Operations Research.* Princeton, N.J.: Van Nostrand-Reinhold, 1978.

Radford, K. J. *Complex Decision Problems.* Reston, Va.: Reston, 1977.

Sassone, Peter G., and William A. Schaffer. *Cost-Benefit Analysis.* New York: Academic Press, 1978.

Tierney, C. E. *Federal Financial Management.* New York: AICPA, 1976.

Tse, John W. D. *Profit Planning Through Volume-Cost Analysis.* New York: Macmillan, 1960.

Wagner, Harvey M. *Principles of Management Science.* Englewood Cliffs, N.J.: Prentice-Hall, 1975.

CHAPTER 7. DEVELOPING ALTERNATIVE SOLUTIONS

Churchman, W. C. *The Systems Approach.* New York: Delta, 1968.

Gordon, William J. J. *Synectics.* New York: Macmillan, 1968.

Koberg, Don and Jim Bagnall. *The Universal Traveler.* Los Altos, Calif.: William Kaufmann, 1976.

Osborn, Alex. *Applied Imagination.* New York: Scribners, 1963.

CHAPTER 8. PRESENTING RECOMMENDATIONS

Nierenberg, Gerald I. *The Art of Negotiating.* New York: Cornerstone Library, 1968.

Royal Bank of Canada. *The Communication of Ideas.* Montreal, 1972.

Woelfle, Robert M. *A Guide for Better Technical Presentations.* New York: IEEE Press, 1975.

CHAPTER 10. EVALUATING THE RESULTS

Weiss, Carol H. *Evaluation Research.* Englewood Cliffs, N.J.: Prentice-Hall, 1972.

Wholey, Joseph S., John W. Scanlon, Hugh G. Duffy, James S. Fukumoto, and Leona M. Vogt. *Federal Evaluation Policy.* Washington, D.C.: Urban Institute, 1970.

CHAPTER 11. SUMMARY

Bolles, Richard N. *What Color Is Your Parachute?* Berkeley, Calif.: Ten Speed Press, 1977.

Crystal, John. *Where Do I Go from Here with My Life?* New York: Seabury Press, 1974.

APPENDIX

Summary of
Some Analytical Techniques

T his appendix provides additional information and a simplified discussion of analytical techniques mentioned in Chapter 6. It is hoped that the practicing consultant or manager can employ this review of the description, use, and advantages of the analytical techniques now available to professionals.

The following discussion is not intended to be a complete description of any technique and some descriptions may even be simplistic. The intended audience for this appendix is not the practicing operations researcher but the consultant or manager who has some analytical skills but may need a general guide to the use of the many techniques currently available.

The order of presentation of material in this appendix is the same order in which the topics were introduced in Chapter 6. The following complete list of topics will help the user locate, in the future, any particular technique description:

1. Qualitative techniques.

    1.1 Basic question.
    1.2 Pattern search.
    1.3 Attribute listing.
    1.4 Forced relationships.
    1.5 Matrix method.
    1.6 Reference projections.
    1.7 Visualize others.
    1.8 Ask other people.

2. Quantitative techniques.

    2.1 Cost analysis.
        (1) Breakeven analysis.
        (2) Incremental cost analysis.
        (3) Opportunity cost analysis.
        (4) Economic life.
        (5) Return on investment.
        (6) Present value.
        (7) Cost benefit analysis.
    2.2 Deterministic models.
        (1) Graph theory.
        (2) Linear programming.

    (3) Networks.

    (4) Integer programming.

    (5) Nonlinear programming.

2.3 Stochastic models.

    (1) Queuing theory.

    (2) Value/utility theory.

    (3) Decision analysis.

    (4) Inventory control.

    (5) Game theory.

    (6) Search theory.

    (7) Simulation theory.

    (8) Dynamic programming.

2.4 Regression analysis.

    (1) Simple regression.

    (2) Multiple regression.

    (3) Econometric models.

2.5 Time series analysis.

    (1) Smoothing.

    (2) Decomposition.

2.6 Time series analysis (Autoregressive/Moving Average, ARMA).

    (1) Box Jenkins.

    (2) Multivariate time series.

2.7 Statistical techniques.

    (1) Descriptive techniques.

        (a) Parametric Tests (F, t, Chi-square)

        (b) Nonparametric (rank order).

    (2) Correspondence techniques.

        (a) Correlation.

        (b) Regression.

2.8 Presentation techniques.

    (1) Graphic.

        (a) Continuous distribution (straight-line, curves).

        (b) Discontinuous distribution (bar, band, step function).

        (c) Noncontiguous (Pi charts).

    (d) Flow chart (PERT, CPM).

    (e) Special format (area diagram, map).

(2) Tabular.

    (a) Frequency distribution.

    (b) Ratio/percentage distribution.

1. QUALITATIVE TECHNIQUES

The qualitative techniques discussed are substantially less well defined than some of the quantitative techniques. Each of the qualitative techniques must be carefully tailored to the particular project requirement, but since the techniques are not rigidly defined, they are easy to shape to each situation.

1.1. Basic Question

The basic question technique consists of analyzing a situation by continuing to ask a series of elemental questions about the subject. These questions normally would be nondirected questions beginning with who, what, where, when, why, and how.

Uses. The basic question method is applicable to almost any problem situation that arises. It is very flexible and the string of questions can lead in any direction of investigation.

Advantages. The principal advantages of this technique are that it is flexible and encourages the consultant to examine the W–H–O–L–E problem before settling into subsets.

For additional reference material see Koberg, 1976.

1.2. Pattern Search

A pattern search is an intuitive review of the facts to determine if an association can be established between two variables. It may be the private thoughts of an individual or the discussion of a group.

Uses. Pattern search is a common approach for projects that lack the time, resources, staff, or data base to conduct more formal analysis. It is a frequently used method of an effective consultant.

Advantages. It is flexible and can easily be applied during periods when it is difficult to do other work. These periods might include driving, riding a bus, or flying.

1.3. Attribute Listing

This approach is more structured than the preceding approaches. It provides a method of subdividing the subject under study by developing categories into which the subject can be broken. These categories are then further defined by descriptors. The descriptors could be used as qualitative measures for the later measurement of alternatives.

Uses. Attribute listing can be an effective technique when you are undecided about how to start your analysis, or if you get into the analysis and get bogged down and need a way to get started again.

Advantages. It is easy to use and can provide a mechanism for generating additional ideas by the project team.

1.4. Forced Relationships

This method of analysis consists of developing comparisons between one situation and another to force an answer regarding the similarities or dissimilarities. This might generate questions such as:

- What differences in management style exist between the eastern division and the western division?
- What are the differences in unit production costs in the two divisions?
- What similar management characteristics does the eastern division have with the leading firm in the industry?

Use. The forced relationship approach can be useful as a "second look" at the analysis after the initial data have been analyzed. The second look may generate broader ideas that may have otherwise been overlooked.

Advantages. The technique frequently can be easily applied and may require no additional data collection.

1.5. Matrix Method

The matrix method permits one set of variables to be arrayed against another set of variables or alternatives. The interrelationships among a number of variables may be sorted and displayed in a matrix.

The matrix provides a guide to structuring the analysis as well as an effective method of displaying the results of the analysis. A typical matrix may have alternative approaches listed on the vertical axis and characteristics listed on the horizontal axis. The results of the analysis are then displayed in the boxes in the matrix.

Uses. The matrix is an effective way to structure and display the performance of alternative systems or parameters.

1.6. Reference Projections

A reference projection is an extrapolation into the future that is made by holding assumptions constant throughout the projection period. Intuition may indicate that the assumption cannot possibly hold constant over the period but the reference projection may indicate that some action must be taken. The execution of the reference projection may include a substantial amount of quantitative data.

Uses. This approach is useful in convincing the client that something must be done. If the reference projection is presented first, the client may then be more receptive to later discussing alternative courses of action.

Advantages. This may be the best approach to convincing the client group that some action must be taken. See Ackoff, 1978.

1.7. Visualize Others

The process of stepping back from the situation in which you are involved and asking yourself how someone else might approach this problem can be an effective analytical technique. You would first recognize that this process may be useful and then select individuals or categories of people that you believe might have insight into the problem.

If you were performing an organization study, you might try to visualize how Peter Drucker would approach this situation.

This technique has some common elements with the Synectics process (Gordon).

Uses. The technique of visualizing what others might do can be helpful when you believe that your analysis is becoming bogged down or that the analysis may be leading you in a direction with which you are not comfortable. This process can also be used when you are looking for some innovative approaches and the project team does not have the experience, creativity, or time to generate them directly.

Advantages. Visualizing what others might do can be an effective way to generate different, and possibly creative, ideas on how to approach a problem.

1.8. Ask Other People

Often it is helpful to ask careful, nondirected questions of people who are not involved in the project. Since they are not involved in the project and you were careful not to give much information in the question, the responses may be unconstrained by the "obvious approaches," the "right answers," or the "acceptable concepts."

By asking questions of people of different professional and social backgrounds you may uncover numerous issues, or approaches, that may not have surfaced.

If you are performing a regional development plan for a North African country you will have urban planners, economists, sociologists, and others on the project team. You may be considering the effect of stabilizing, or incentives to stabilize the movement of nomadic herdsmen. If you asked a microbiologist, "What parameters would you suggest be included in an analysis of stabilizing the nomadic herdsmen in North Africa?" you probably would receive some substantially different insight into the study.

Uses. The process of asking questions of people outside the project can be used on most projects with little expenditure of time or resources. The many irrelevant responses can be recorded and not considered further.

Advantages. This method provides an efficient way to get fresh ideas that are unconstrained by the client situation or the project team background.

2. QUANTITATIVE TECHNIQUES

Quantitative analysis includes a multitude of techniques for handling numerical data. The techniques discussed in this appendix are some of the most commonly used in management consulting.

2.1. Cost Analysis

As the name implies, cost analysis includes several techniques for handling a subset of numerical data, money. Some techniques are discussed below.

BREAKEVEN ANALYSIS

Breakeven analysis is a tool that addresses the volume-cost relationships by considering the interaction of fixed costs, variable costs, and revenues.

Uses.   Breakeven analysis can be used:

- To help establish a proper volume of operation for a product.
- To analyze the marginal contribution of a product.
- To evaluate the expected impact on profits of an increase in plant capacity.
- To evaluate the effect of a make or buy decision on profits.
- To analyze the impact of holding workers at the lower end of a cyclical production cycle.
- To analyze the impact of utilizing overtime labor to increase production output.

Advantages.   Breakeven analysis is a relatively easy way to look at volume cost relationships that can yield very useful insights into the project.

Constraints.   Care must be exercised when breakeven analysis is used for discrete functions within an organization since the allocations of costs among units may not be very accurate. Moreover, the analyst should remember that all costs tend to become variable in the long run, so the development of fixed and variable costs should be based on the time frame for the decision being considered.

INCREMENTAL COST ANALYSIS

Incremental (or differential) cost analysis focuses on the costs that vary with any of the alternatives being considered. The costs that probably will not vary from alternative to alternative will not be included in the analysis. Thus the conclusion can be made on the "net effect" on costs rather than on total costs.

Uses. This analytical technique is often used for such applications as a make or buy decision for a part in a manufacturing firm. In this circumstance, factory overheads, material costs, procurement costs, and procurement overheads may be relevant costs. However, such costs as selling expenses and corporate general and administrative expenses may not be relevant costs for the analysis.

Advantages. The principal advantage of incremental cost analysis is to simplify the analysis by including only those costs that are relevant. This makes the analysis easier to structure, less expensive to collect data for, and easier to understand.

Constraints. Care should be used in selecting the costs to include and the costs to exclude from the analysis. As with most cost analysis, care should be exercised when including any allocated, or prorated, accounting charges. In a make or buy decision, if the part were purchased from outside the floor space formerly used for manufacturing the part would be saved. However, this does not necessarily mean that the costs of the floor space would be saved. As a general rule, unless there is a change in actual costs, the changes in prorated accounting costs should usually be disregarded.

OPPORTUNITY COST ANALYSIS

The opportunity cost to be considered for an investment decision is the return that could be obtained by placing the investment amount under study in an alternative investment.

Uses. This approach can be used for any investment decision to establish a minimum amount for the expected return of a potential project. For instance, if you are considering a project that would require $1,000,000 of capital and the company could earn 10 percent interest on the capital in bonds, certificates of deposit, and the like, the annual opportunity cost of the returns forfeited by funding the project would be $100,000. This cost should be considered as a minimum amount that the potential project must earn to be worthwhile.

Advantages. The concept of opportunity cost provides a mechanism for considering the broader base of choices available to the decision maker.

ECONOMIC LIFE

The useful economic life of an asset is a major factor in investment decisions. The economic life may be considered in three elements. These are:

- Technological life.
- Market life.
- Physical life.

The working period until the asset is obsolete is quite short in technologies that are dynamic and, of course, would be longer for mature technologies. An example of machines and processes having a technological life shorter than physical or market life is the electronic "chip" or large-scale integration industry. New processes must be adopted because technological innovations have made it difficult to compete with the last generation process.

The market life has an impact on investment decision because the disappearance of a market may end the useful life of a piece of equipment even though it is technologically competitive and physically operable. An example of this may be an automated buggy whip manufacturing machine. In the coming decade, much of the United States' capacity for producing large automobiles may see an end to its economic life as a result of an end of its market.

The physical life of a process or equipment is the period of time until the unit fails completely or the periodic repair costs justify the termination of its use.

Use. The concept of economic life can be useful when the entry into a new manufacturing process is being considered. The concept may be useful on any investment decision involving real income-producing assets.

Advantages. Another vantage point may be gained regarding the returns or risks of an investment by analysis of economic life.

RETURN ON INVESTMENT ANALYSIS

The return on investment (ROI) method of cost analysis provides a capability for comparing the expected savings or increases in income with the value of the initial investment. This comparison is usually expressed as a percentage.

There are many types of ROI analysis available. The type used should be tailored to the client situation and to the type of analysis to be performed. Some of the types commonly used are:

- *First year.* Consider only the first year undiscounted rate of return. If this return is satisfactory, then the return in future years will increase since the outstanding investment will be periodically reduced by the amount of the annual depreciation.
- *Multiyear.* The returns are calculated for each year of the expected useful life of the investment.
- *Average year.* Since a part of the investment will be recovered each year through depreciation, the average value of the outstanding investment is one-half of the total. The use of this average value will double the stated ROI rate.
- *Discounted cash flow.* The savings, or increases in income, in future years and the string of investment costs are discounted to reflect the fact that income, or costs, in future years does not have the same impact as it would at the current time. These future incomes and costs would be discounted to the present by an appropriate rate of interest (possibly the cost of borrowing for a private firm) and the percentage ROI obtained.

Uses. The return on investment approach is widely used to analyze investment strategies in private organizations.

Advantages. The ROI technique can incorporate the economic life of the asset, the discounted stream of income and costs, and provide a comparison of the return versus the investment in easily remembered percentages.

PRESENT VALUE ANALYSIS

Present value techniques are used to discount incomes and costs that occur in different time periods so that the incomes and costs can be compared based on their value at time zero.

Two of the most commonly used formulas for calculating present value are as follows:

- The present value (PV) of a payment (P) occurring n periods in the future at interest rate i would be obtained from

$$PV = \left(\frac{1}{(1 + i)^n} \right) P$$

- The present value of a constant stream of payments for n periods at interest rate i may be found from

$$PV = \left(\frac{(1 + i)^n - 1}{i(1 + i)^n} \right) P$$

The factor would be multiplied by the payment amount to obtain the present value.

Uses. The present value technique can be used for investment decisions to obtain a discounted dollar comparison of the options.

Advantages. Present value techniques are particularly useful for decisions that must be made during periods of national or international high interest rates. As interest rates rise, investment decisions can change character quickly as the value of future income diminishes quickly. The basic formulas can be programmed into personal calculators or microcomputers for easy use, but present value tables are available in many publications.

COST BENEFIT ANALYSIS

Cost benefit analysis is the process of estimating the net benefits (benefits minus costs) associated with the alternatives for achieving a defined goal. Cost benefit analysis is most often applied to projects in the public sector. The common decision criteria used for cost benefit analyses are:

- *Net present value.* All estimated costs and benefits are discounted at an appropriate discount rate to obtain a composite present value. The higher the net present value, the more desirable is the project.

- *Cutoff period.* A specific time period is selected and the estimated benefits must be greater than the estimated costs over this period. All benefits and costs beyond the cutoff time are disregarded.
- *Payback period.* The length of time that the project will take for its estimated benefits to pay back its estimated costs is used as the decision criterion. Normally, no discount rates are used.
- *Benefit to cost ratio.* The benefit to cost ratio is the ratio obtained by dividing the discounted benefits by the discounted costs.

Uses. The cost benefit analysis approach has been used for many years in judging the relative future merits of public projects and thus as a basis for funding alternative projects.

Advantages and Disadvantages. The cost benefit approach is an effective tool for public, and sometimes private, decision making. The net present value decision criterion is generally believed to be the most accurate in assessing a project's worth.

The cutoff period method seldom is used because it disregards anything beyond the cutoff period and because the choice of the length of the cutoff period can be difficult.

The payback period is also infrequently used because it can disregard high-value returns that may be otained later than the initial cost was paid back.

The benefit to cost ratio can yield questionable results for projects with smaller costs because the measure is discounted benefits per dollar of discounted costs. The benefit cost ratio can be a very useful approach to selecting several projects when there is a limit to the available capital that precludes the funding of all the projects.

2.2. Deterministic Models

Models that do not include factors whose values are represented by probability functions are generally said to be deterministic. For a given set of inputs to a model the outputs are definable. Since deterministic models do not contain random phenomena, they are often easier for management to understand and use.

Many types of deterministic models are in use. Some are described below to provide an overview of the substance and use of these models.

GRAPH THEORY

Graph theory is composed of a variety of approaches for representing the relationships among sets of objects or factors. It is not an integrated theory. Thus the graph, a collection of points and lines connecting points, may be used to display the many properties of a subject under study.

Graph theory includes many approaches such as:

- Traditional lines plotted on X and Y coordinates.
- Bar charts.
- Arrow diagrams to indicate interrelationships among the most important elements of a system.
- Forrester-type diagrams for displaying business or industrial process aplications (see Robertshaw, 1978).
- State approach for describing the status of physical systems over time (see Robertshaw, 1978).

Uses. The uses of graph theory are extensive and the listing of uses below will further clarify the foregoing definition. The uses include:

- Information system flow diagrams.
- Wiring diagrams.
- Organization charts.
- Economic theory.
- Scheduling charts.
- Financial analysis.
- Genetics charts.
- Architectural design.
- Trajectories of moving objects.

Advantages. Graph theory includes many approaches to visualizing and communicating a concept or the relationship among variables.

For an excellent discussion of graph theory, see Moder (1978).

LINEAR PROGRAMMING

Linear programming (sometimes called linear optimization) is made up of several techniques for finding where a linear function of several variables assumes an extreme (or. optimum) value. The variables are usually subjected to constraints presented as linear equalities or inequalities.

The linear programming model is usually subject to the assumptions of:

- Divisibility, where the total inputs and the related profit are proportional to the level of output.
- Additivity, when the total use of resources by all activities is the sum of the individual uses.
- Nonnegativity, since no variable (or activity) can be negative quantity.

Uses. The uses of linear programming include the following:

- Product mix, the allocation of resources among the many processes and end uses in an organization to optimize profits.
- Feed mix, the selection of an optimum quantity of multiple feed grains for feeding livestock.
- Investment analysis, to determine the overall impact of an alternative solution on the company's operations so that a more accurate return on investment can be developed.

Advantages. The use of linear programming permits optimum values to be determined for problems with numerous variables and constraints. In many instances, linear programming techniques, with the use of computers, are the only practical method to solve a problem (see Moder, 1978; Wagner, 1975).

NETWORK MODELS

Network models are a special case of linear programming models that have mathematical features that permit major efficiencies in finding optimum solutions. Since the network models may contain thousands of activities and hundreds of constraints, the models, combined with automated processing, allow solutions to be found that would otherwise be difficult or impractical.

Uses. The major uses of network models are for transportation problems of finding the shortest route or the lowest-cost route and for product distribution problems matching demand and supply from a series of warehouses or plants. The uses include:

- The distribution of products from points of manufacture to storage locations to minimize total production and distribution costs.

- The analysis of multiple plant locations when products are manufactured at a number of plants.
- The distribution of empty freight cars from their existing locations to new locations in a manner that minimizes transportation costs.
- The distribution of material to ships and the dispatching of ships to ports of call for a multipoint shipping network.

Advantages. The network model is effective for those problems having large numbers of activities and constraints. The model can provide optimum choices when no other approach is practical (see Wagner, 1975; Moder, 1978).

INTEGER PROGRAMMING

Integer programming is closely linked with combinatorics. Integer programming is a subset of linear programming in which all the variables are integers (whole numbers).

Uses. The uses of integer programming include resource allocation, facilities planning, and job shop scheduling (see Moder, 1978).

NONLINEAR PROGRAMMING

Nonlinear programming includes those techniques used to analyze problems where the variables cannot be described by linear relationships. The techniques may include those that are unconstrained and those that are constrained. Those that are constrained may face linear constraints or nonlinear constraints (see Moder, 1978).

2.3. Stochastic Models

A stochastic, or random, process is a group of randomly occurring variables. The various methods of handling these random variables has led to the development of many mathematical techniques. These techniques include:

- The simple random walk whereby the change in the variable can only be ± 1.
- Recurring events that describe the distribution of events until the starting value is again obtained.
- The Markov chain describing a situation in which there is a finite number

of states and the change from one state to another is affected by the transition probabilities for going from one state to another.

- The Poisson distribution, usually used to describe those events that occur over a continuous scale, such as time.
- .The renewal process, used to describe the random nature of the life of an item or its replacement rate per unit time.

The types of models that the foregoing techniques are applied to are described in the following paragraphs.

QUEUING THEORY

A queue, or waiting line, is a group of items requesting service at some service entity. The items in the queue may be people, telephone calls, vehicles, and so on. Normally the items to be served are called the "customers" and the entity providing the service is called the "server."

The major parameters by which queues are described are:

- The input process (how the customers arrive).
- The queue discipline (the way the customers are served after they arrive).
- The service mechanism (the number of customers served at once, the number of servers, type of service, duration of service).

Queuing theory provides a method of predicting the amount of waiting time in a queue or the length of the queue. These predictions can be useful in the analysis of operations and processes.

The principal limitation of the practical use of queuing theory is that current formulations for standard mathematical distributions often do not match the actual distribution of arrival and service rates in real problems. Nonstandard distributions increase the mathematical complexity.

Uses. The uses of queuing theory include:

- Determining the number of personnel required to keep customer waiting times below a management-defined limit. This would include the number of tellers needed in a bank, the number of telephone operators on duty, or the number of attendants at a gasoline station.
- Determining the number of machines or equipment to provide for a system. This would include the number of telephone lines to be leased for an

airline reservation service, the number of fare gates at a subway station, or the number of pumps at a gasoline station.

- Determining work processes. This would include predicting the number of machines that a single operator should operate.

Advantages. Queuing theory is very helpful in simulating an existing or a planned process to be able to evaluate the impact of alternative courses of action (see Moder, 1978; Wagner, 1975; Martin, 1972).

VALUE/UTILITY THEORY

Value theory is the theory used to describe preferences and utilities. It provides a theoretical foundation for the techniques used to describe and measure preferences and permit preferences to be described quantitatively for use in decision analysis.

Preference theory involves (1) the description of a set of decision alternatives, or courses of action, and (2) the development of a preference or indifference relation for each alternative set.

Value theory incorporates probability distributions for each set of strategies. The theory also permits certain criteria, parameters, or characteristics to be introduced (see Moder, 1978).

DECISION ANALYSIS

Decision analysis (DA) is an approach for dealing with uncertainty in decision making. It is similar to value theory in that it provides a structured method of incorporating the preferences of the decision maker. DA is based on including the decision maker's judgment about the outcomes from alternative strategies and the decision maker's preferences on these alternative strategies.

It is guided by a set of axioms, which generally include:

- Relative preferences.
- Quantification of preferences.
- Transitivity.
- Comparison of lotteries.
- Quantification of uncertainties.
- Substitutability.
- Equivilence of conditional and unconditional preferences.

Uses. Decision analysis can be applied to problems such as:

- Situations with uncertain results in differing time periods.
- Situations involving many intangibles such as good will, political impacts, and public image.
- Situations with several objectives that may be in conflict with each other.
- Situations involving several decision makers whose preferences will differ.
- Situations like those that frequently occur in large institutions, where the impact of the decision will be felt by many groups.

Advantages. The use of decision analysis permits the decision maker to act consistently in accordance with his or her preferences (see Moder, 1978).

INVENTORY CONTROL MODELS

Inventory control models provide a theoretical framework for assisting management to decide:

- When to replenish the stock.
- How much of the stock to obtain at one time.

The models would typically include:

- The demand and supply of the stocked item. The stock clerk must anticipate next week's production requirement and the wholesaler must project the sales level of the retailers he serves.
- The reorder cost (or setup cost) for processing another order.
- The cost of holding the stocked item in inventory.
- The penalty cost (or lost profit) for running out of the item.

Inventory models can be single period models (newsstand stocking) or they may be stochastic continuous models that incorporate probabilistic demand functions and the effect of various lead times.

Uses. The uses of inventory control models are widespread in industrial and commercial levels. Such models are applied to the decisions on procuring and stocking parts for manufacturing organizations as well as for stocking the shelves in retail stores.

Advantages. Inventory control provides a consistent, profit-based measure to guide management decisions in setting inventory levels.

GAME THEORY

Game theory is a collection of techniques used to describe the choices available to people in "gamelike" situations. The game is usually described by an extensive form, which is a tree with nodes and connectors between nodes, and a normal form, which is the relationship that determines the vector of the expected payoff to each group of strategies.

The game uses strategies, which are rules that tell the participant what to choose at each information set.

Game theory includes several types of game in the major categories of:

- Zero-sum two-player games.
- Nonzero-sum two-player games.
- Multiple-person games.

Uses. The uses of game theory have expanded rapidly since World War II when significant developments were made. The uses include:

- Economic applications such as product strategy and trading horses.
- Military strategy for analysis of alternative action plans.
- Psychological applications for such activities as bargaining and political science.

Advantages. Game theory provides a somewhat rigorous framework to analyze uncertainty for applications not well suited for other techniques (see Moder, 1978).

SEARCH THEORY

Search theory is planning for and implementing an approach to looking for a target. The theory has received substantial attention during and since World War II. The following factors must be considered in search theory:

- Motion of the searcher.
- Type of area search (random, parallel sweeps).

- Optimum resource allocation.
- Target motion.
- Evasion by the target.

Uses. The uses of search theory include developing plans and procedures for searches for:

- Military targets such as ships and submarines.
- Ships or aircraft during rescue missions.
- Police hunting for fugitives.

Advantages. The use of search theory can help minimize the time required to find a target, maximize the probability of finding a target, and minimize the resources required to find it (see Moder, 1978).

SIMULATION THEORY

Simulation is generally accepted to mean the use of numerical computation in a mathematical model to obtain estimates of the probability of some specified actions. Statistical sampling is a key element in simulation.

Most problems complicated enough to deserve modeling will require the use of a computer to process the numerical calculations. The model is constructed using probabilistic statements for some parameters, and then pseudorandom numbers are generated so that a distribution of possible outcomes is generated.

Uses. Simulation is used for a large number of applications such as:

- Manufacturing processes.
- Physical phenomena.
- Biological phenomena.

Advantages. The advantages of simulation are that estimates can be obtained for those functions for which there is no straightforward mathematical solution. Also, the use of simulation is often easier than some more rigorous mathematical techniques that might be used. Although simulation models are approximate and empirical, they can be used for many applications.

DYNAMIC PROGRAMMING

Dynamic programming is generally defined as a set of techniques used to analyze sequential decision processes. It may be used in a deterministic or a stochastic model. The techniques used for computation include:

- Backward optimization.
- Successive approximations.
- Linear programming.

The central theme in dynamic programming includes:

- The acceptance of states.
- The characteristics of states.
- Embedding of solutions.
- Functional equations.
- Principle of optimality.
- The local income function.

Uses. The uses of dynamic programming include inventory control, travel models, and managing a research project. Any application that included sequential decision making might use dynamic programming (ses Moder, 1978; Wagner, 1975).

2.4. Regression Analysis

Regression analysis is widely used in the management sciences and in econometrics. It consists of using the past relationships between identified independent parameters and a dependent variable of interest to predict the future behavior of the dependent variable.

Since data are required to establish the past relationships, the use of regression analysis can be costly. For this reason, regression is often used for those situations where the accuracy desired is worth the expense of collecting the data.

Regression analysis will provide a measure of the association between (or among) the variables. Much care should be exercised in concluding that causal relationships exist.

This discussion of regression is divided into three parts:

- Simple regression.
- Multiple regression.
- Econometric models.

SIMPLE REGRESSION

Simple regression analysis consists of examining the relationship between one independent variable and one dependent variable to determine the historical relationship between the two. These historical data are used to develop an equation that best describes the relationship. The equations may be of the following types:

- Linear:

$$y = a + bx$$

- Exponential:

$$y = ae^{bx}$$

- Logarithmic:

$$y = a + b \ln x$$

- Quadratic:

$$y = a + bx + cx^2$$

- Cubic:

$$y = a + bx + cx^2 + dx^3$$

The accuracy with which the selected equation matches the historical data is indicated by a factor called the coefficient of determination (r^2). The values of r^2 range between 1.0 (good fit) and 0 (poor fit).

These formulas may be used to predict future values of the dependent variable (y).

Uses. The uses of simple regression analysis include:

- Sales forecasting.
- Projection of physical phenomena such as pressure/volume data.
- Real estate price projection.

Advantages. Simple regression provides a method of establishing a trend line based on historical data. Simple regression is somewhat easier to perform than other types of regression.

MULTIPLE REGRESSION

In multiple regression there is one dependent variable to be predicted but there are two or more independent variables. The general formula used for multiple regression is

$$y = a + b_1 X_1 + \cdots + b_j X_j$$

The equation is a linear equation. There are numerous techniques available to convert nonlinear relationships to fit the general linear equation.

Uses. The uses of multiple regression are numerous since many variables are influenced by more than one factor. These uses include:

- Sales forecasting.
- Production costs.
- Process throughput time.

Advantages. Multiple regression can help establish the relationship between a number of independent variables and a dependent variable (see Makridakis and Wheelwright, 1978).

ECONOMETRIC MODELS

Many situations are too complex to be represented by a single regression formula. One way to represent these more complex situations is through the use of a family of multiple regression formulas. These systems of simultaneous multiple regression formulas involving several interdependent variables are usually called econometric models.

Uses. There are several uses of econometric-type models but the best known use is in forecasting elements of interest of the economy based on a large number of inputs of such independent variables as income, population, and employment.

Advantages. Econometric modeling is essentially the only practical way of handling the relationships of complex interrelated systems (see Makridakis and Wheelwright, 1978).

2.5. Time Series Analyses

This type of analysis, as the name implies, includes approaches for analyzing factors against time as a base. The two approaches summarized are:

- Smoothing.
- Decomposition.

These techniques are frequently used because they are reasonably easy to use and not too expensive to maintain.

SMOOTHING

Smoothing is the process for determining a line or a curve through the historical data that permits the cycles and random errors to be averaged out. Thus predictions can be made based on this "average" trend. Smoothing is similar in concept to plotting a set of data points and "eyeballing" an average through the data points and drawing a trend line.

The smoothing techniques commonly used include:

- Moving averages.
- Exponential smoothing.
- Adaptive control method.
- Harmonic smoothing.

Uses. Smoothing techniques are widely used on situations such as:

- Sales forecasting.
- Inventory demands.
- Failure rates.

Advantages. It is fairly simple to set up and maintain the data necessary to operate a smoothing model for forecasting purposes. The accuracy may be rough but the cost is low (see Makridakis and Wheelwright, 1978).

DECOMPOSITION

The use of decomposition involves the breakup of the data to separately identify and describe the major subpatterns. This could include a separate identity for the:

- Seasonal pattern.
- Trend pattern.
- Cycle pattern.

plus leveling out the random characteristics of the data.

Thus each of the patterns would be separately forecast and the resulting forecasts would be recombined.

The techniques commonly used for decomposition include:

- Moving average.
- Ratio to moving average.
- Trend analysis.
- Census II method.
- FORAN system.

Uses. Decomposition techniques are used for making forecasts as well as for examining the trends, cycles, and seasonalities of the data. These techniques are widely used in business and in economics for such applications as predicting:

- The business cycle.
- Stock market prices.
- National economy.
- Industrial production.
- Interest rates.
- Commodity or service demand.

Advantages. Although some people believe that there are theoretical weaknesses in the decomposition method, it has been successfully used for half a century to predict certain types of activity. It is relatively easy to do and the concept is readily understandable (see Makridakis and Wheelwright, 1978).

2.6 Time Series Analysis (Autoregressive/Moving Average, ARMA) Models

The autoregressive/moving average (ARMA) methods are similar to the other time series approaches, smoothing and decomposition. The ARMA methods use historical time series data to develop a baseline for predicting future activities. The approach used in the ARMA methods to identify the patterns is substantially different from the approaches used in smoothing and decomposition.

The two approaches mentioned in this appendix are:

- Box-Jenkins.
- Multivariate time series.

BOX-JENKINS

The name Box-Jenkins describes the approach consolidated by the two authors to describe invariate time series ARMA models.

The Box Jenkins method emphasizes the proper use of autocorrelation and partial autocorrelation coefficients of the data to provide appropriate factors for the general ARMA equation. Automated techniques are necessary for situations of any complexity. ARMA models develop the seasonal, trend, and cyclical patterns in the data and provide a way to forecast future activity levels.

Uses. The Box-Jenkins method could be used on many types of data, including:

- Regional sales forecasts.
- Manufacturing productivity.
- Subway passenger volumes.

Advantages. While a substantial amount of automated manipulation of historical data is required, and some trial and error may be necessary, forecasting accuracies can be better than for other approaches for some situations (see Box and Jenkins, 1976).

MULTIVARIATE TIME SERIES

Multivariate ARMA (MARMA) models are similar to the Box-Jenkins ARMA models except that the MARMA models deal with more than one variable or time series.

In addition to the techniques used in the ARMA models, the MARMA models use a cross-autocorrelation to identify the degree of association, for different time lags, of the values of the dependent variable and the values of the independent variable.

Uses. Since the MARMA approach is new, extensive practical experience is not yet available. It could be used for:

- Sales forecasting.
- Production output forecasting.

Advantages. It permits two or more variables to be examined against the historical data (see Makridakis and Wheelwright, 1978).

2.7. Statistical Techniques

Statistical analysis is used extensively in business and government. The intention of this section is to mention and define several concepts used in statistical analysis.

Statistics are generally separated into descriptive statistics and statistical inference (inductive statistics). These categories will be summarized after some basic statistical terms are defined.

The entire population of the topic of interest is designated as N. A subset of the entire population is called a sample and is designated as n. Most people have selected some items (the top apples in a bushel) and made a decision about the quality of the entire population. This is usually called judgment sampling.

Statistical sampling is a more precise method of assembling a representative group of objects. The two principal approaches to statistical sampling are:

- Random sampling, where each sample of that size is equally likely to be drawn from the universe.
- Systematic sampling, where the first item (B) is selected from the universe in a random fashion and then the next items are selected by a repeating factor (R) such that the samples are $B, B + R, B + 2R$, and so on. Unless the universe is random, this sampling will not be random.

The mean of the items considered is the sum of the items divided by the number of entries. This is commonly called the arithmetic average. The mean of a population is called μ (mu) and the mean of a sample is called $\bar{x}$.

A measure of the variation of the data around the mean is called the standard deviation. The standard deviation of a population is called σ (sigma). The standard deviation of a sample is indicated by s.

Other statistical descriptions sometimes used are the median (where approximately half of the items are higher and half the items are lower than the median item) and the mode (the most frequently occurring item).

DESCRIPTIVE TECHNIQUES

Descriptive statistical techniques include measures of location and measures of variation. The measures of location include the:

• Mean.
• Median.
• Mode.

The measures of variance include:

• Variance.
• Standard deviation.

In addition to these measures, there are other ways to describe data. Some of these are discussed below as parametric tests and nonparametric tests.

Parametric Tests. Parametric testing implies that the variable is related to an equation that will yield a distribution of outcomes with changes of the variable. Parametric tests include F, Student t, and Chi-square tests.

• *F tests.* The F test is a variance ratio defined as

$$\frac{\text{estimate of variance } (\sigma^2) \text{ based on variability of } \bar{x}_s}{\text{estimate of variance } (\sigma^2) \text{ based on variability within samples}}$$

  If F is large the null hypothesis must be rejected. This test is commonly used in the analysis of variance.
• *Student t.* The Student t distribution is a technique for developing confidence intervals for characteristics of small samples.

- *Chi Square (χ^2) Distribution.* The Chi Square tests are a measure of the agreement between the observed frequencies and the expected frequencies for a situation. If the difference is small, we may accept the null hypothesis. If chi square is large, the null hypothesis will be rejected or judgment deferred.

Nonparametric Tests (Distribution-Free). Nonparametric tests are generally defined to be those where the population does not conform to a normal distribution and where no hypotheses were made about specific values of parameters. Nonparametric tests include:

- *Rank Correlation.* When working with large sets of paired numbers, the calculation of the correlation coefficients can be difficult. (With the widespread use of microcomputers this difficulty may be reduced.) Useful results can sometimes be obtained by using the rank of the data observations rather than the actual data. Thus the coefficient of rank correlation (r') can be calculated and used to test for significance.
- *Sign Test.* It is sometimes useful as a short cut to use a sign test. Each positive or negative sign attached to changes in the data is examined. The number of plus and minus signs can then be used in testing a null hypothesis about the data.
- *Rank Sum.* This technique can be used with two samples. The samples will be jointly ranked and the rank of each data point in the combined sample will be identified. The null hypothesis is then used to test for significant differences among the ranks of the two samples.
- *Trend Significance.* The significance of a trend in a set of data points can be tested by determining whether each point is above or below the median for the data set. The data array is then reviewed to determine the runs of the lower values or the higher values. A null hypothesis is used to determine if the number of runs (consecutive data points on the same side of the median) is significant and thus whether a trend is significant.

CORRESPONDENCE TECHNIQUES

Correspondence techniques suggest types of approach that provide an indication of the relationship between sets of variables. Two widely used correspondence techniques are correlation analysis and regression analysis.

Correlation. For a set of data (X_i, Y_i) the dispersion of the data points around a line of regression is influenced by the degree of dependence of one variable on the other. The greater the dependence between the variables, the smaller the variation of data points around the line of regression will be.

A measure of the degree of dependence between the variables is called the coefficient of correlation (r). This coefficient is a measure of the association between two variables.

For some series of data the proportion of the variance of Y that is related to X is called the coefficient of determination (r^2).

Regression.   Regression analysis was described earlier.

2.8. Presentation Techniques

The results of most analyses can be enhanced by effective presentation techniques. Some of the more common techniques listed here are intended to be used as idea generators for an analyst faced with a presentation requirement. The two principal categories are graphic and tabular.

GRAPHIC

The graphic displays provide a pictorial or schematic representation of the concept or results to be communicated. There are many types of graphic display. Some of them are illustrated below.

Continuous Distribution.   The continuous distribution graphic displays include straight lines and curves.

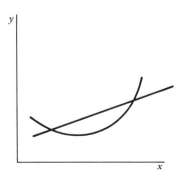

Discontinuous Distribution. The types of display in this category are bar charts, band charts, and step functions.

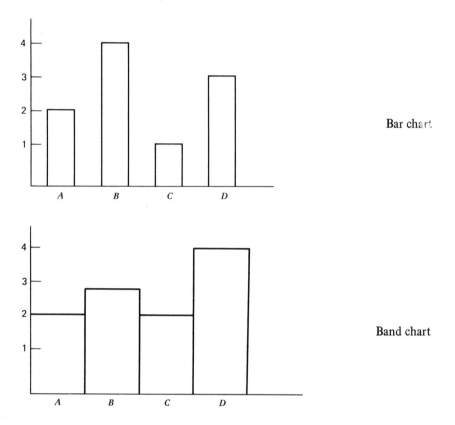

Bar chart

Band chart

A special case of the band chart is the histogram, where measurements are grouped on the horizontal scale and the class frequencies on the vertical scale.

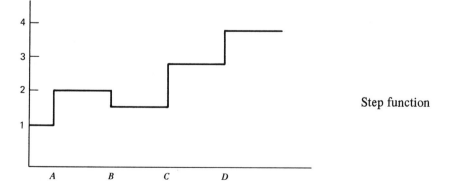

Step function

Noncontiguous. Noncontiguous displays are often effective. An example of a noncontiguous display is a pie chart.

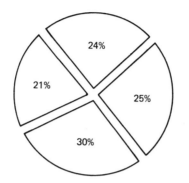

Pie chart

Flow Chart. A flow chart links a series of actions (or other relationships) in a manner that provides a structure to the interrelationships. The charts used in PERT and CPM are popular examples of flow charts.

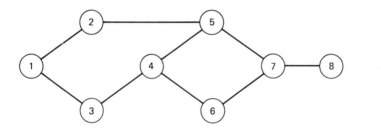

Flow chart

Special Formats. Additional formats include geographic maps with selected highlighting and area diagrams. Area diagrams are sometimes called Venn diagrams.

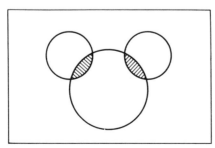

Area diagram

TABULAR

There are many ways to display the data generated in your analysis in a tabular form. Some of the more common techniques are as follows.

Frequency Distribution. The frequency distribution is a listing of the occurrence of the items as measured in some interval.

Year	Number of Hits
1970	123
1971	150
1972	185
1973	162

Ratio/Percentage Distribution. The ratio or percentage distribution is simply a listing of the proportion of some total related to each independent variable.

Player	Percentage of Total Points
Tall	40
Fast	30
Strong	20
Short	8
Slow	2

This appendix has briefly summarized a number of analytical techniques and provided references for many of the techniques. The listed references are those that I consider useful for that topic.

Index